Berlioz

Unlocking the Masters Series, No. 34

Series Editor: Robert Levine

Unlocking the Masters

The highly acclaimed Unlocking the Masters series brings readers into the world of the greatest composers and their music. All books come with audio tracks taken from the world's foremost libraries of recorded classics, bringing the music to life.

> "With infectious enthusiasm and keen insight, the Unlocking the Masters series succeeds in opening our eyes, ears, hearts, and minds to the greatest composers"—Strings

Series Editor: Robert Levine

Ravel: A Listener's Guide, by Victor Lederer, 2000
Richard Strauss: An Owner's Manual, by David Hurwitz, 2000
Verdi: The Operas and Choral Works, by Victor Lederer, 2000
The Mahler Symphonies: An Owner's Manual, by David Hurwitz, 2004
Decoding Wagner: An Invitation to His World of Music Drama, by Thomas May, 2004
Exploring Haydn: A Listener's Guide to Music's Boldest Innovator, by David Hurwitz, 2005
Dvorak: Romantic Music's Most Versatile Genius, by David Hurwitz, 2005
Getting the Most Out of Mozart: The Instrumental Works, by David Hurwitz, 2005
Getting the Most Out of Mozart: The Vocal Works, by David Hurwitz, 2005
The Great Instrumental Works, by M. Owen Lee, 2006
Opera's First Master: The Musical Dramas of Claudio Monteverdi, by Mark Ringer, 2006
Shostakovich Symphonies and Concertos: An Owner's Manual, by David Hurwitz, 2006
Chopin: A Listener's Guide to the Master of the Piano, by Victor Lederer, 2006
Sibelius Orchestral Works: An Owner's Manual, by David Hurwitz, 2007
Beethoven's Symphonies: A Guided Tour, by John Bell Young, 2008
Puccini: A Listener's Guide, by John Bell Young, 2009
Schubert's Theater of Song: A Listener's Guide, by Mark Ringer, 2009
Liszt: A Listener's Guide, by John Bell Young, 2009
Schubert: A Survey of His Symphonic, Piano and Chamber Music, by John Bell Young, 2009
Bach's Choral Music: A Listener's Guide, by Gordon Jones, 2009
Bach's Keyboard Music: A Listener's Guide, by Victor Lederer, 2010
Beethoven's Piano Music: A Listener's Guide, by Victor Lederer, 2011
Bernstein's Orchestral Music: An Owner's Manual, by David Hurwitz, 2011
Beethoven's Chamber Music: A Listener's Guide, by Victor Lederer, 2012
Richard Strauss: An Owner's Manual, by David Hurwitz, 2014
Verdi: The Operas and Choral Works, by Victor Lederer, 2014
Ravel: A Listener's Guide, by Victor Lederer, 2015
C.P.E.: A Listener's Guide to the Other Bach, by David Hurwitz, 2016
Schumann: A Listener's Guide, by Victor Lederer, 2017
Listening to Handel: An Owner's Manual, by David Hurwitz, 2019
Listening to Mendelssohn: An Owner's Manual, by David Hurwitz, 2020
Bach's Operas of the Soul: A Listener's Guide to the Sacred Cantatas, by Mark Ringer, 2021
Beethoven's Orchestral Music: An Owner's Manual, by David Hurwitz, 2021
Berlioz: A Listener's Guide, by Victor Lederer, 2021

Berlioz
A Listener's Guide

Victor Lederer

AMADEUS PRESS

Lanham • Boulder • New York • London

Published by Amadeus Press
An imprint of The Rowman & Littlefield Publishing Group, Inc.
4501 Forbes Boulevard, Suite 200, Lanham, Maryland 20706
www.rowman.com

6 Tinworth Street, London SE11 5AL, United Kingdom

Copyright © 2021 by The Rowman & Littlefield Publishing Group, Inc.

All rights reserved. No part of this book may be reproduced in any form or by any electronic or mechanical means, including information storage and retrieval systems, without written permission from the publisher, except by a reviewer who may quote passages in a review.

Book design and composition by Snow Creative

Library of Congress Cataloging-in-Publication Data

ISBN 978-1-53813-558-7 (paperback)
ISBN 978-1-53813-559-4 (e-book)

For Zoe

Contents

Acknowledgments   ix

Chapter 1. Berlioz, Musical Dramatist and Experimenter   1

Chapter 2. Early Symphonic Masterworks and a Flop:
The *Symphonie fantastique;* Byron, Paganini, and *Harold*;
the *Symphonie funèbre et triomphale*   11

Chapter 3. The Concert Overtures   25

Chapter 4. Berlioz the Shakespearean   31

Chapter 5. Goethean Drama: *La Damnation de Faust*   49

Chapter 6. Sacred Music, Part 1: The Rediscovered
Messe solennelle, the *Te Deum* and *L'Enfance du Christ*   67

Chapter 7. Sacred Music, Part 2: The Requiem
(*Grande Messe des morts*)   85

Chapter 8. Dramatic One-offs: *Cléopâtre, Lélio,*
and *Benvenuto Cellini*   97

Chapter 9. *Les Troyens*, Virgil (. . . and Shakespeare)   115

Chapter 10. Summer Nights   149

Chapter 11. Listening to Berlioz   163

Notes   165
Selected Bibliography   169
Track Listing   171

Acknowledgments

Thanks to the usual family members: Elaine, Paul, Karen, and Kate, plus two new ones, Eli and Zoe. Thanks as always to Bob Levine, who's as good at this now as when we started working together fourteen years and nine books ago. Thanks to Bernie Rose for suggesting the topic, which turned out to be far more challenging—and exhilarating—than I imagined.

Berlioz: Musical Dramatist and Experimenter

Although he was one of the seminal figures in the romantic movement, Hector Berlioz's musical legacy is laden with paradox. Nearly every major work by Berlioz can baffle and even displease on first hearing. Further acquaintance may reverse that, or it may not. His style is so individual, restless, and dramatic that some find it exhausting. But without question, while acknowledged as a major figure in nineteenth-century music and a seminal figure in the romantic movement, he can be problematic.

A quick look at his oeuvre reveals a variety of forms, including two symphonies, of which the *Symphonie fantastique* is by far the most performed of his works. Although not the first piece of program music, meaning that it has a narrative, and neither standard in form nor content, it's surely the most influential. There are three operas and four drama-driven sacred works by this decidedly nonreligious man of the world. Six concert overtures, of which two are popular and appreciated, represent his style at its most approachable, though these, too, are wild and restless creations. Perhaps most characteristic of Berlioz's passions and ambitions are the two hybrids of symphony and drama, one based on *Romeo and Juliet*, the other on *Faust*. Clearly, Berlioz was preeminently a composer of musical drama under various guises. Even the song cycle *Les Nuits d'été*—Summer Nights—although quieter than anything else, is no less intense in its affective depictions of the six poems chosen. In fact, they're as restless as anything else by Berlioz, and immensely influential on composers who copied this first orchestral song cycle. *L'Enfance du Christ*—The Childhood of Christ, which he called a "sacred trilogy"—contains much that's dreamlike and sweet, but also long passages that vividly depict the anxieties and terrors of such disparate biblical characters as the virgin mother Mary and the wicked but tormented King Herod. The point is that Berlioz is preeminently, and perhaps exclusively, a composer of musical drama, no less than his great contemporaries (and friends) Verdi and Wagner. With a few notable exceptions, no two of his works are alike, each an experiment of some sort.

A passionate reader with a critical mind, Berlioz was always in search of material that fired his imagination, so it makes some sense here to group the works by literary source. We'll look at his two large-scale works based on Shakespeare (the early dramatic symphony *Roméo et Juliette* and the late opera *Béatrice et Bénédict*) together. Although as noted not religious, he grasped as well as any composer the drama inherent in sacred music, particularly on display in the Mass for the Dead—the Requiem. Since there was always a market for sacred works in nineteenth-century France, Berlioz seized every opportunity to compose in those forms as they presented themselves. His major work, the opera *Les Troyens*—The Trojans—is based on the *Aeneid* of Virgil, another lifelong obsession. The grouping works well enough until we get to three compositions that are important but difficult to classify by source, so they wound up together. Of these Berlioz's first opera, *Benvenuto Cellini*, is the most significant.

Berlioz was a prolific music critic and writer on music—so prolific, in fact, that there's not enough room in a listener's guide like this for a complete survey of those aspects of his career, and they must be summarized at the end of the chapter. One of his major writings is an autobiography that's entertaining and popular as composer's memoirs go, if of questionable accuracy. Since his eventful and interesting life and career have been covered in detail elsewhere, there's room only for presentation in passing here.

There are different ways of saying this, but everyone who listens carefully to Berlioz comes to this conclusion: "His imagination is quite unlike that of any other composer."[1]

Berlioz was as French as they come, never even learning to speak English, his first wife's native language. But if you attempt to compare or reconcile his musical style to others such as Fauré, Debussy, Ravel, or Poulenc—whose works sound identifiably "French"—you'll realize that the French style is not his: Berlioz sounds only like himself. And although influential on many of them and admired and copied by his more avant-garde contemporaries, the effects of composers he learned from (Gluck, Mozart, and Beethoven) are generally less obvious in his music. In this respect, he may parallel another contemporary and friend, Chopin, who forged his own inimitable style out of bits of this and that and a daring and original imagination.

To look at Berlioz's music first from the widest perspective: all his major works blend drama and descriptive music. One of his main aesthetic goals was to stimulate a visual response. The mysterious but undeniable ability of sound to evoke a picture in the mind has been a tool employed by almost every composer, including the most revered. The greatest names have employed "pictorialism" or tone painting, with Renaissance masters using rising melodic figures in church music to describe a heavenward ascent, just as Berlioz does in the Requiem. A fugue from J. S. Bach's *Well-Tempered Clavier* or the opening movement of one of Beethoven's string quartets employs musical techniques that express emotion—joy, sorrow, or a sense of struggle are common and readily perceived—but these works do not generally suggest a picture in the mind of the listener. Nor, as abstract music, are they supposed to. But when Beethoven imitates birdcalls or a thunderstorm in his "Pastorale" Symphony, his goal is to make the listener "see" the birds and the rain. Having his music create visual images is one of Berlioz's chief goals, particularly in the early symphonic works and the concert overtures. *Benvenuto Cellini*, his earliest opera, is also remarkably pictorial, with the approach of a carnival crowd rendered convincingly in carefully gauged increases in dynamics—volume—to cite one example among hundreds. His responsiveness and love of the pictorial carries through in later works, too. Among his later works, *L'Enfance du Christ* is particularly vivid in this respect.

That Berlioz is a preeminently a dramatic composer is obvious as well. There are the familiar symphonies of his early maturity (the *Symphonie fantastique* and *Harold en Italie*), and three operas that are by definition music dramas. All his sacred works, from the early *Messe solennelle* to the musically complex Te Deum of 1855, are packed with dramatic renderings of their sacred texts, with the Requiem the most dramatic of all. Perhaps his two most characteristic works, *La Damnation de Faust* and *Roméo et Juliette*, display his purpose unambiguously. In both, he recasts classical dramas that have inspired him into his own forms. It's worth noting that they're subtitled, respectively, *Légende dramatique* and *Symphonie dramatique*. Throughout his career, he excelled at setting text, a crucial skill for a composer of music drama. Yet paradoxically, this ability may come through most clearly in the least overtly dramatic of his major works, the song cycle *Les Nuits d'été*. Its close depiction of the lyrics is confessional and thus essentially dramatic as well.

Many will be surprised to learn that, alone among the important composers, Berlioz did not compose at an instrument or even play one seriously, preferring to let his imagination take the lead:

> When I think of the appalling quantity of platitudes for which the piano is daily responsible—flagrant platitudes which in most cases would never be written if their authors had only pen and paper to rely on and could not resort to their magic box—I can only offer up my gratitude to chance which taught me perforce to compose freely and in silence and thus saved me from the tyranny of keyboard habits, so dangerous to thought, and the lure of conventional sonorities, to which all composers are to a greater or lesser extent prone.[2]

He did play the flute, guitar, and timpani, none typical fodder for a master of orchestral writing like him. Most composers of his time played the piano, but Berlioz didn't want to learn the instrument, which, as he stated, inevitably created a result that pulled toward the piano's sound and layout. Given the scale, complexity, and color of his works, it seems astonishing that he conceived them without touching an instrument, but so it is. Yet it's one of those mysteries of genius that may be less than mysterious to academically trained musicians. Mozart played several instruments and did most of his composing at the keyboard, but seems to have been capable of imagining music and writing while away from an instrument.

In fact, there's more method to musical composition than many realize, with the key variables being melody, rhythm, harmony, and the means of delivery—whether voice, a solo instrument, or ensemble—in countless possible combinations. The potent influence of music on our nervous systems leads us to imagine there's more in the way of wild inspiration, not just these few factors, complex and difficult as the composer's work may be.

A late starter as a professional musician, Berlioz attended the Paris Conservatoire, the country's leading institution for musical training, as prestigious as the Curtis Institute or the Juilliard School are in the United States today. There, he was trained in the basics, of which counterpoint (also called polyphony or part-writing) is one of the fundamentals. To define counterpoint inadequately but in a way that may help here, it's the way different melodic lines interact. Although independent-minded and often combative, Berlioz graduated from the Conservatoire, winning its biggest award, the Prix de Rome, so he clearly learned well whatever they wanted to teach. But Berlioz's allergy to the piano may have come at a cost to his compositional technique.

Surely part of what makes Berlioz so different is how he imagined his music. Some love that peculiarity while others never get used to it, with a long-running dispute about his sound the result. What follows is a simplified summary of that dispute, describing the composer's technical deficiencies. These function at a textural level not everyone may hear, let alone grasp, but may explain some of the difficulty some experience when listening to Berlioz.

"And consider Berlioz. With all his clumsiness and his bad basses, he succeeds in making the tempestuously romantic impression he strove for. In France we do not set 'I love you' in invertible counterpoint. Berlioz owes his genius to his spontaneity."[3] The "bad basses" cited by the conductor Charles Munch refer to the lowest strand of Berlioz's part-writing, which don't always follow the rules of counterpoint and harmony he was taught at the Conservatoire. This has been explained by musicologists in a couple of different ways. The sharp-witted Brit D. F. Tovey wrote that the methods by which Berlioz was trained at the Conservatoire were weak, and that "whenever Berlioz makes what seems manifestly a mistake, every attempt to correct it substitutes for something characteristic something impossibly banal."[4] Charles Rosen, an American musicologist and pianist, explained it slightly differently, suggesting that Berlioz would indeed have smoothed out his counterpoint and harmony if he'd learned to work his ideas out on the piano, which as we've seen he refused to learn. In Berlioz's era, most composers played the piano, and for them Bach's *Well-Tempered Clavier* was the chief tool for instruction in composition. Thus, Berlioz might have learned "the contrapuntal realization of harmony in a purely practical way—by playing Bach."[5] Alert to the paradoxes of Berlioz's style, Tovey's point is that it might also have deprived the world of some quirky but characteristic sounds and inspirations. Rosen admired Berlioz greatly if with reservations,[6] and Munch, one of the greatest Berlioz conductors, punted.

Berlioz has a singular, readily identifiable sound that can be analyzed in different ways. There's the dashing, sometimes frenetic quality that grabs your attention from the start, or nearly so. A familiar piece like *Le Carnaval romain*—the Roman Carnival Overture—opens with an attention-grabbing phrase full of rising intervals but also rhythmic compressions that are Berliozian signatures; but within twenty seconds, he's moved to a quiet melody for the English horn, one of his favorite instruments but one that's not normally prominent. Typically for him, too, the yearning English horn melody is phrased with an irregularity that's fascinating and part of Berlioz's appeal. Other great composers, such as Schumann and even Beethoven on occasion, get stuck in an all-too-regular pattern of statement-and-reply, or sometimes in Schumann's case, just straight, tedious repetition of a melodic phrase. Hating what's predictable, Berlioz avoids this sort of phrasing if he possibly can. His melodies are longer and far less regular than those of almost any other major composer. A certain high-strung, upward-reaching gesture, usually expressing agitation, is another of the composer's signatures. Only Berlioz does it, and no one else.

To stay with the Roman Carnival Overture, once the long passage where the English horn leads is over, a livelier, dancelike section begins. Leaving aside for a moment the brilliance of the orchestration, this section is filled with nearly continuous rhythmic alterations and compressions, far more than just accenting a weak beat here and there. These stumbling, tripping, heart-stopping explosions have a manic, proto-Stravinskian energy and force. The composer also liked certain unusual time signatures, notably 9/8, which he makes more varied use of than anyone. He experimented repeatedly with deploying different meters to be played simultaneously. To obtain a primitive or barbarous effect in *L'Enfance du Christ*, he has the orchestra switch repeatedly between alternating beats, anticipating (and probably clearing ground) for the twentieth-century master Bartók.

Going back as far as the Renaissance, most of the composers whose music holds up well are restless and experimental in their harmonic practice, trying to work in as much dissonance—the sound of tones that clash to the ear—as possible. Dissonance is a potent expressive device that, when skillfully employed, makes music more interesting for both composer and audience. In this regard, Berlioz enjoyed its effect often to shade and color. You'll notice in the second part of the overture that he makes almost continuous shifts of harmony, some as subtle shading, but others, particularly in the closing phrases, more violent, multiplying the force of the rhythmic eruptions. In *La Damnation de Faust*, the composer portrays its protagonist's dissatisfaction and unease more subtly but no less effectively with nearly continuously shifting harmony. The late operas (*Les Troyens* and *Béatrice et Bénédict*) are variously described as more classical, restrained, and musically conservative than the wild early works, but both are rich with expressive dissonance.

Berlioz wrote a treatise on instrumentation, and, of course, he's a great practitioner, though not necessarily showy. In addition to the English horn, he liked other orchestral underlings, notably the viola and cello in preference to violins, and was from early in his career a skilled composer for percussion instruments, a group that he amplified, differentiated, and which he endowed with great subtlety. Here, for example, Berlioz's influence on Ravel seems clear, as the large, delicate and varied percussion section in that master's great ballet *Daphnis et Chloé* must be drawn from Berlioz's practical lessons.

To return to counterpoint for a moment, Berlioz is uneven in his practice of this craft. In some places, such as the fugue in the last movement of the *Symphonie fantastique*, he comes up with exciting, percussive cadences that clarify the entries of the fugue subject, a technique Verdi copies in the closing section of his Requiem.[7] The somber fugue that opens *Harold en Italie* is beautiful and effectively sets the stage for the entire work. On the other hand, passages where he ostentatiously combines two ideas contrapuntally, as in the "Bal des Capulets" in *Roméo et Juliette*, are coarse and ultimately less effective. Thus, there's really no hard-and-fast judgment to be made about his varied approaches to polyphony.

Some will be surprised to learn just how much self-borrowing Berlioz did, recycling thematic material he liked. This was a common practice in the baroque era; both Bach and Handel recycled their own material regularly. There's nothing wrong with this, as it was all the product of the composer's intellect. As we'll see, what's curious and often funny is how different some of it sounds in the later context. Of all his works, the *Messe solennelle* of 1824 and rediscovered in 1991 (see page 67) turned out to be his most productive source, with seven vivid ideas recurring in later works, including *Benvenuto Cellini*, its offspring the Roman Carnival Overture, the *Symphonie fantastique*, the Requiem, and the Te Deum.

Berlioz is not a perfect composer, and some of his obvious flaws include lapses in taste, of which there are a few, of varied character. To cite one, the setting of Confutatis maledictis—Silence the accursed—from the Requiem is so jolly that it sounds like a college football cheer: get 'em, tigers! There are more, which we'll note as we hear them. He lacked judgment about proportion, too, and *Benvenuto Cellini* is the worse for it, stuffed (indeed, overstuffed) with great material though it is. In fact, Berlioz never quite perfected large-scale organization, with even his last major work, the two-act *Béatrice et Bénédict*, out of balance in crucial ways, as we'll see. Like *Cellini*, it's full of good stuff. Sometimes his organizational problem manifests itself as a tendency to lose focus and sprawl, perhaps most noticeably in the Requiem and *Les Troyens*. These moments may be defined as a sense of puzzlement, when as listener you may find yourself wondering where the music is and where it's going.

Perhaps best in terms of quality of material and organization of the larger-scaled compositions are the well-known and appreciated symphonic works of the composer's early maturity, the *Symphonie fantastique*, *Harold en Italie*, and *La Damnation de Faust*. The mosaic-like *Faust*, made up mostly of short musical segments, has a playing time of two hours and is rarely dull, though it's imperfectly organized. Berlioz's best in terms of consistent quality are the song cycle *Les Nuits d'été* and the concert overtures *Le Carnaval romain* and *Le Corsaire*—The Corsair. Also in this league are the overtures to *Benvenuto Cellini* and *Béatrice et Bénédict*, often performed on their own—certainly more than either rarely heard opera.

Leaving aside its groundbreaking role as the first song cycle with an orchestral accompaniment, *Les Nuits d'été* is remarkable for showing a more subtle side of the composer. Using a small orchestra, Berlioz treats these lyrics of love and loss with his usual sensitivity to the meanings—overt and hidden—of the texts, which call for delicacy rather than thunder. The lyrical side of his style is on luxuriant display, with all his melodic and structural quirks completely in place and enjoyable. It's short, tight, and brilliantly sequenced.

The three overtures are more flashy, but with playing times of eight to ten minutes Berlioz never loses his way, keeping the surprises fresh, even once we know the music well. All but *Béatrice et Bénédict* follow the same structural pattern, with an arresting opening phrase or two followed by a relatively long lyrical passage at a slow tempo. They then pick up speed, breaking themes into dazzling fragments carried on tides of accelerating rhythm and harmonic shocks. And in these his orchestral mastery is proudly on display.

Berlioz's productive, passionate, not-too-happy life has been covered well. His own memoir, while witty and fascinating, was written over the course of decades and has been shown to contain much that's inaccurate. Some errors can be attributed to faulty memory, others to malice. He's funnier and more self-deprecating than you might expect, though. The relatively unbiased biography by the Berlioz scholar David Cairns completed in 2000 is definitive and readable but, in two big volumes, probably too long for all except the most deeply interested. D. Kern Holoman's 1989 biography is shorter, and also informative if more technical about the music. Unfortunately, there's not much in the way of middle ground, but the essentials of his biography can be read in summary in Ted Libbey's *The NPR Listener's Encyclopedia of Classical Music* or the *Oxford Dictionary of Music*. Since new facts and even major compositions by Berlioz (such as the *Messe solennelle*, which turned up in 1991) continue to emerge, it's a good idea to stay current if he and his music interest you.

Berlioz was at least as productive as a writer as he was as a musician. According to his *Memoirs*, he took up criticism to supplement his income and to help clean up the Parisian music scene: "What a weapon I would have for defending the beautiful and attacking whatever seemed to me opposed to it! There was also the consideration that it would add a little to my income, which was still very meagre."[8] At a low point in his career in the late 1840s it looked as though he would have to abandon composition and make his living as a writer and critic alone. This turned around with the composition of *L'Enfance du Christ*, which returned him to moderate popularity.

In an exaggerated but ultimately truthful way, Berlioz tells us that writing was painful:

> It is a struggle to get myself to begin to write a page of prose, and before I have done a dozen lines (except on very rare occasions) I get up, pace the room, stare out of the window into the street, pick up the first book that comes to hand, in short do anything to fight off the boredom and fatigue which rapidly descend on me . . . Musical composition is a natural activity for me and a pleasure, prose writing a burden.[9]

This is a charming description of the procrastination all writers experience, and a demonstration of just how fluent and gifted a writer he was. And remember, he wrote the librettos for his last two operas. A number of the reviews have been collected in an anthology, *Evenings with the Orchestra*.

Berlioz's most significant written contribution in terms of the craft of music is the *Grand Traité d'instrumentation*—The Great Treatise on Instrumentation, published in 1843 and soon translated into several other languages. Although he didn't play an instrument, he understood their capacities and knew many of their players well. Although beyond the range of this short survey, this practical guide has influenced contemporaries, including Wagner, and musicians who followed. Richard Strauss, a later orchestral master, revised it. Strauss commented that Berlioz was "full of ingenious visions, whose realization by Wagner is obvious to every connoisseur."[10]

Early Symphonic Masterworks and a Flop
The *Symphonie fantastique*; Byron, Paganini, and *Harold*; the *Symphonie funèbre et triomphale*

Symphonie fantastique

There's a great deal of interesting background and myth regarding the *Symphonie fantastique*, one of the seminal works in the Western musical canon. Hoping to impress a beautiful Irish actress, Berlioz completed his first version of the work in 1830, revising it thoroughly over the next fifteen. Berlioz and the alarmed Harriet Smithson were married for nineteen mostly unhappy years, but the world is infinitely richer for his initial obsession. The composer's autobiography is not always accurate, and for students of his music, it's less than helpful. For instance, later discoveries have shown that several large sections (the fourth-movement march from the unfinished opera *Les Francs-Juges*[11]) as well as important musical themes (the opening lament and the beloved's motif that runs through and animates the work, and the main melody of the third movement) were lifted from earlier works, none of which borrowings the composer mentions.

Berlioz copies Beethoven's programmatic concept expansion to five movements from four, from that master's Symphony No. 6 (the "Pastorale") as well as Beethoven's manner of trying out thematic ideas before settling on others (this in Berlioz's finale, borrowed from the last movement of Beethoven's Symphony No. 9). But uncertainties and distortions surrounding its creation and influences pale in the face of its boldness of conception and the brilliance of execution. Here the young master has triumphantly steered the form to a new type of his own making, the symphony as internal drama.

The composer's written program for the work and each of its five movements are well known but bear repeating:

> *A young musician of unhealthy sensitive nature and endowed with vivid imagination has poisoned himself with opium in a paroxysm of love-sick despair. The narcotic dose he had taken was too weak to cause death but has thrown him into a long sleep accompanied by the most extraordinary visions. In this condition his sensations, his feelings and memories find utterance in his sick brain in the form of musical imagery. Even the beloved one takes the form of melody in his mind, like a fixed idea which is ever returning and which he hears everywhere.*

First Movement: Visions and Passions

At first he thinks of the uneasy and nervous condition of his mind, of somber longings, of depression and joyous elation without any recognizable cause, which he experienced before the beloved one had appeared to him. Then he remembers the ardent love with which she suddenly inspired him; he thinks of his almost insane anxiety of mind, and his raging jealousy, of his re-awakening love, of his religious consolation.

This tumultuous movement (Track 1 of the accompanying online audio) opens with a dreamlike introductory passage that occupies about one-third of its roughly fourteen-minute playing time. Delicate breaths from the flutes and French horns lead to a long, lamenting phrase Berlioz wrote early in his career. This leads with an unexpected energy to skittering figures for the violins over nervous jabbing for the horns. The first of many sighs and weeping figures appear in the violins; a restless figure for the horns is also the first of many that will appear throughout the work. Falling plucked strings lead, finally, to a quick explosion, which preceded the main theme—the idée fixe—that drives the work.

Sung by the flutes and violins, this looping melody—consisting of long-held notes alternating with shorter ones, returning over and over to the same pitch, aptly depicting the shy nobility of the beloved as well as the narrator's obsession—is underpinned by strange grunts in the lower strings that suggest agitation or perhaps the carnal side of his excitement. More low figures for the strings will appear throughout the *Symphonie fantastique*. In any case, this thematic complex is one of the great melodic inspirations by Berlioz or anyone. In fact, while the sonata form (exposition, development, and recapitulation) for an opening movement of an instrumental work of the classical era is present, it's of far less import than the convulsive surges alternating with calmer, more reflective, or sometimes somber passages that drive this music along. But the idée fixe is always in or near the foreground. Also, unlike a work from the classical era, Berlioz doesn't supply a contrasting theme; the musical battle is between phrases of the melody or the moods in which it's cast. The listener seems more to be following a narrative or listening to a personal confession in musical form than following the intellectual argument of sonata form. The melody is finally carried on a big, excited climax for the full orchestra. The religious mood mentioned in the description is set to reverent-sounding chords that seem a bit theatrical; it's probably good to remember that there's an ironic distance between Berlioz himself and the volatile protagonist of his symphony.

Second Movement: A Ball

In a ball-room, amidst the confusion of a brilliant festival, he finds the loved one again.

Perhaps the most straightforward section of this rich, allusive, and wild work, the second movement is still a long way from simple, eventually but inevitably finding its way under one's skin. Set as a light-footed waltz, it follows the pattern of many such movements by serious composers in the nineteenth and twentieth centuries, including Weber, Chopin, Schumann, Mahler, and perhaps most significantly Ravel, whose orchestral masterpiece *La Valse* opens with a similar passage in which the listener seems to approach the ballroom, hearing the dance first from afar. There are two versions of the movement, in one of which Berlioz added an extended part for solo cornet that ultimately seems like overkill; performances without it work better.

Shuddering strings and sweeping arpeggios for the harp at low volume set the stage. The waltz theme is the idée fixe, spun out into a dance by means of fiddly elaboration, punctuated by woodwinds and two harps, which have a prominent role throughout the movement. At one point, though, the unaltered beloved's melody appears, played by the flute and oboe, accompanied by excited grunts in the lower strings. The fiddly version of the theme returns, irresistible in its choreographic drive. But everything pauses for a dreamlike, slow iteration of the idée fixe for the clarinets delicately decorated by the harps. The driving coda only seems conventional, but fragments of the main theme are woven in and the composer's eruptive rhythms give it exceptional energy and personality.

Third Movement: In the Country

It is a summer evening. He is in the country musing when he hears two shepherd-lads who play the ranz-des-vaches *(the tune used by the Swiss to call their flocks together) in alternation. This shepherd duet, the locality, the soft whisperings of the trees stirred by the zephyr-wind, some prospects of hope recently made known to him, all these sensations unite to impart a long unknown repose to his heart and to lend a smiling color to his imagination. And then she appears once more. His heart stops beating, painful forebodings fill his soul. "Should she prove false to him!" One of the shepherds resumes the melody, but the other answers him no more . . . Sunset . . . distant rolling of thunder . . . loneliness . . . silence.*

Influenced by Beethoven's "Pastorale" and influential on Mahler (perhaps most obviously in the second movement of his Symphony No. 7, which opens with a similar dialogue, there between French horns), this spacious slow movement follows the composer's scenario closely, giving less repose than the rustic setting might suggest, and differing completely in mood from Beethoven's calm andante. It's also the section that gave the composer the most trouble and which took longest to revise.[12] It's set by Berlioz basically as an extensive prologue and postlude flanking an episodic main section. An effective bit of tone painting, the opening section a consists of a gentle dialogue between oboe and English horn, which, as described, imitate alpine shepherds calling each other across valleys on their horns. The main section consists of a long-spun theme followed by five episodes. Long, slow, and very quiet, the postlude is remarkable for its careful writing for four timpani and, again, the English horn; but it may be the composer's chief miscalculation in the *Symphonie fantastique*, coming as it does at the end of this already extended movement.

The opening passage, exquisitely written for winds and trembling strings, beautifully evokes vast space and unhurried leisure. The main theme, sung by violins and flutes, based on a gracefully rising scale figure, was adapted by the composer from the *Messe solennelle* of 1824. Five variation-like episodes follow, differing in character, with the second, for instance, being quite agitated. Here, however, the idée fixe appears recognizably though broken into phrases over violent commentary from the strings. The third episode beneath beautiful melodic writing for the clarinets features busy activity for the strings that unsettles the superficially relaxed mood, and effectively portrays the narrator's agitation. The idée fixe appears again, broken but recognizable in the fifth episode, where the timpani, sounding as distant thunder, depict the natural world as opposed to the dreamer and his fantasies. These take over as the movement ends in a very leisurely and quiet passage. One has to give Berlioz credit for seeing his vision for the movement though without compromise and executed beautifully, too; but the postlude, which takes almost three minutes' playing time at the end of this fifteen-minute movement, goes on a bit for some listeners. The fourth movement livens things up, however.

Fourth Movement: The Procession to the Stake

He dreams that he had murdered his beloved, and that he has been condemned to death and is being led to the stake. A march that is alternately somber and wild, brilliant and solemn, accompanies the procession . . . The tumultuous outbursts are followed without modulation by measured steps. At last the fixed idea returns, for a moment a last thought of love is revived—which is cut short by the death-blow.

Now the musical narrative takes off in this great, macabre section which could only have been written by Berlioz but also had immense influence on Mahler in his many march-based songs and symphonic movements. Consisting, as described, of a grim-jawed march with wild interjections, the howls (in the spinning figure for the violins) and laughter of the crowd are clearly depicted. There's a compressed, hard-driving climax and just before the end, a single, haunting iteration of the idée fixe by the clarinets. A sharp chord for the full orchestra depicts the drop of the guillotine blade, followed by two plucked notes for the strings as the dreamer's head bounces into the basket, a grotesque but irresistibly funny inspiration.

As you can tell, this is a remarkable section that will make a big impression on first hearing and is easy to appreciate and even enjoy in its singular blend of excitement, terror, and humor, which the composer carries through in the finale. It's worth paying attention to the instrumental writing, which is heavy but always clear. That for the percussion is carefully conceived and remarkably effective. Berlioz makes much of the grotesque sounds bassoons can produce, and lower brass get a workout, too.

Fifth Movement: The Witches' Sabbath

He dreams that he is present at a witches' dance, surrounded by horrible spirits and monsters in many fearful forms, who have come to attend his funeral. Strange sounds, groans, shrill laughter, distant yells, which other cries seem to answer. The beloved melody is heard again, but has its noble and shy character no longer; it has become a vulgar, trivial and grotesque kind of dance. She *it is who has come to attend the witches' meeting. Friendly howls and shouts greet her arrival . . . . She joins the infernal orgy . . .*
Bells toll for the dead . . . a burlesque parody of the Dies irae *. . . the witches' round dance . . . the dance and the* Dies irae *are heard at the same time.*

One of the wildest rides in the classical repertory, the "Witches' Sabbath" is an immense outpouring of energy that's also staggeringly clever. It opens in eerie harmonies and strange orchestral colors leading to a dance rhythm iterated by the flutes, followed by the beloved's theme, now heard as a coarse dance, responded to in roars of delight by the full orchestra, representing her fellow witches, who know her well. As we'll see, one of Berlioz's strengths is the unpredictability of his melodic phrasing. Here he casts the theme as squarely and vulgarly as possible, bleated out by the woodwinds, brayed back faithfully—and squarely—by the larger ensemble. Tolling chimes introduce the theme from the Catholic requiem Mass known as the Dies irae—"day of wrath," Judgment Day as described in the Latin text—here blared out in long notes by bassoons and tuba, which then alternate with cackling in dance rhythm for the high strings and winds. Here he tries out different themes before settling on one, in Beethoven's manner. This builds excitement for the rip-roaring dance theme, the "witches' round dance," that begins in the strings. (These energetic fugal entries are what Verdi imitated in his Requiem.) There are rises and falls in volume and orchestration, but the astonishing energy is never allowed to flag. Finally, the witches' round and the Dies irae are combined. There's an eerie passage where strings tap their bows against the strings while the woodwinds trill, in an early but striking show of the composer's genius as an orchestrator. In the movement's climax and coda, the themes enter in close succession, with the beloved's last, now set as the maddest cancan, at once hilarious, horrifying, and grand.

Byron, Paganini, and *Harold en Italie* ("Harold in Italy")

Equal to the *Symphonie fantastique* in quality and appeal, this four-movement work also has an interesting backstory. Berlioz wrote it on a generous commission from the great string player Niccolò Paganini (1782–1840). Primarily known as a violinist, Paganini was also a virtuoso on the viola and guitar. In late 1833 or early the following year, the two met in Paris; Paganini asked Berlioz to compose a work for viola and orchestra. Berlioz felt that Paganini, a competent composer who had a far better feel for the instrument, should write it himself. Paganini insisted; Berlioz sketched a work in which the solo viola does not appear throughout. Moreover, the viola part wasn't virtuosic enough for Paganini, who protested and never played it, though he did pay generously for it. Berlioz thought to expand on what he had done for Paganini, using Byron's long poem "Childe Harold's Pilgrimage" as an inspiration and a loose framework. His own experience in Italy also influenced the end result.

George Gordon, Lord Byron (1788–1824), is with Paganini (and Berlioz) another remarkable nineteenth-century creative type. Born noble but poor, Byron came into wealth and title when a remote cousin died, leaving him as heir. He died in Greece while attempting to unite factionalized rebels against the Ottoman Empire that then ruled that nation. Byron's death drew the attention of Western Europe to the plight of Greece, which, with outside help, broke away from Turkish domination in 1832. His influence on Western culture has been vast since his death. Byron's long poems and dramas are respected more than they are read. But his shorter lyrics, of which "She Walks in Beauty" is probably the best known, are concise and direct, speaking readily to short modern attention spans. His most important legacy is the conception of the "Byronic" hero, actually an antihero, much admired by generations up to and including today as an irresistibly appealing protagonist who is impulsive and passionate, yet defiant of authority and filled with self-doubt too. (All of which seem to have been Byron's own traits.) His influence on nineteenth-century music was considerable, with this work of Berlioz probably its finest large-scale example. Schumann and Tchaikovsky both composed works based on his verse drama *Manfred*; two lesser-known Verdi operas (*I due Foscari* and *Il Corsaro*) are based on dramas by Byron, with Corrado, the pirate-hero of the latter, another typically "Byronic" hero. And the same drama and character also served as the theme for Berlioz's great *Le Corsair* overture. Schumann and others composed songs to his shorter poetry.

Published in 1812, "Childe Harold's Pilgrimage" is the poem that made Byron famous. This long (five hundred-plus-page) verse narrative is semi-autobiographical, relating the travels of a young man who is already disillusioned in search of distraction and room to reflect, and hungry for new experience in his journey. Like most literate Europeans Berlioz was an admirer of Byron; having traveled in Italy himself, the composer made his own connections and uses for Byron's poem, the Paganini commission, his own recent past, and something new he needed to express. In any case, this work surely has far more of Hector than Harold.

Berlioz quotes Paganini, describing his viola as "an admirable Stradivari."[13] Although any instrument by Stradivarius is an object of beauty, the viola itself is a back-bencher in the musical world and little known or understood outside. Looking pretty much like a violin only bigger, the viola has a deeper pitch and darker tone than the fiddle. Lacking the penetrating brilliance of the violin's high notes or the rich depths of the cello, its relegation to musical purgatory is unfortunate; the viola can sound as interesting as its fellow strings when well played, as by the great twentieth-century violist William Primrose, to name perhaps its most acclaimed performer. Solo pieces for viola are rare, with *Harold* its most famous example; there's also a good concerto by Bartók. The viola's main role in orchestral works is to provide harmonic background or reinforce the violins above or cellos below. The instrument is more noticeable in a string quartet, but its role is typically similar, acting as a timbral glue between the two violins and cello. A few composers—notably Mozart, who loved to play the viola, and Brahms—give the instrument greater prominence in some of their chamber works. Berlioz adored its dark tone, making great use of it here as well as in *La Damnation de Faust*.

Since it's set in four movements like a standard symphony of the classical or early romantic periods, it's probably fair to call *Harold en Italie* the most conservatively structured of Berlioz's major works. Yet it remains utterly individual in its layout and sensibility. The overall form of the movements is: fast (following a long, slow introduction)–slow–fast (the scherzo)–followed by a quick-tempo finale. Again, like Beethoven's "Pastorale" and his own *Symphonie fantastique*, each movement of *Harold* carries a descriptive title. Berlioz stitches the whole work together with a theme presented at the beginning by the viola, which serves to represent Harold in his various moods. The solo writing is never showy (which is what Paganini objected to originally)—it's no concerto for viola. Sometimes the viola engages in in intimate dialogues with other soloists or small groups of instruments that remind one more of chamber music than a symphony. Berlioz again copies the finale of Beethoven's Symphony No. 9 in his last movement by having themes from earlier in the piece recalled then rejected, before moving to an exciting conclusion that is, however, unlike Beethoven's Ninth or even his own *Symphonie fantastique*. *Harold* stands apart as a noble example of program music and, typically for Berlioz, a dramatically charged musical structure.

The first movement, subtitled "Harold in the Mountains—Scenes of melancholy, happiness and joy," opens with a long, somber fugato (fuguelike) passage that begins in the lower strings, to which the woodwinds and French horns add moaning commentary. The winds intone the Harold theme, here in a majestic, staking rhythm. Finally, the viola—accompanied by the harp, soon joined by the clarinets—presents the lilting melody, solemn, tender, reflective, and noble in long notes, which soon opens out into more a flowing phrasing. (This theme was lifted whole from the *Rob-Roy* overture, where it's played by the English horn, another favorite instrument of the composer's.) The melody is then repeated and decorated ecstatically by the full orchestra. Following a quizzical comment from the strings and high woodwinds, a pendant to Harold's theme in this movement slips in almost backhandedly, first in the orchestra, then more hesitantly, almost as if it's stammering, by the solo viola. This tune, equally memorable and more infectious than the Harold melody, also moves more steadily and has a more outward-looking urbanity. There's even a tail that dances happily along, and its every appearance is welcome. The pendant receives some agitated treatment, but the sense of the movement is mostly joyful and eager to dash ahead in Berlioz's best manner. The composer lightens texture and speeds up for the long closing passage—the coda. This begins in the lower strings, to which woodwinds and French horns add their voices in thematic fragments. There's a big climax that shows Berlioz at his best and most characteristic, with unexpected rhythmic eruptions and exciting compressions of the melodic material.

Beethoven casts a benign shadow over the second movement, "Procession of pilgrims singing the evening hymn." Like the second section of that master's Symphony No. 7, it's a slow movement that's not too slow, with Berlioz using the using the same tempo (allegretto), the same 2/4 beat at a marchlike pulse. They share a coolness of tone and have similar, hypnotic effect. But the details of the two are of course quite different. Berlioz's march opens as if heard from afar, with plucked tones from the harp, orchestral violas, and double-basses and quiet, interestingly dissonant chords for the French horns and bassoons. Soon the steady hymnlike march enters quietly in the violins. But since, as we know, Berlioz dislikes and avoids overly regular phrasing, he adds an irregularly pulsating tail for the French horns and woodwinds that perhaps suggests an outdoor echo; Tovey hears "muttered prayers."[14] The viola enters with the Harold theme, sung in long notes as a quiet commentary. The composer weaves all the material together hauntingly before lowering the volume and turning more earnest with what he describes in the score as the "*Canto religioso*." Here, between long, choralelike chords above and the hymn melody way below in the double-basses, the solo viola begins a long passage of arpeggios (broken chords) that follow the overall harmonic movement but show, too, that the protagonist is apart, watching rather than participating in the scene. The magical coda recapitulates the material, but in fragments and at ever lower volume.

The third movement, "Serenade of an Abruzzi mountaineer to his sweetheart," functions as the scherzo, which literally means "joke" in Italian but in a classical composition denotes a lively movement at a quick tempo. It's usually placed second or third in a four-movement work. Perhaps the most conventional of *Harold*'s four, the serenade also more or less follows the ABA pattern typical of the instrumental scherzo, although with this composer's individuality always present. This character piece opens with a dance rhythm in the strings, over which a memorable tune is heard played by the piccolo and oboe. This is barely given time to settle in before there's a slowdown to half-speed as the rocking serenade tune is played by the English horn with the clarinet adding burbling accompaniment. The solo viola with its companion the harp soon joins in with the thoughtful Harold melody; woodwinds add interesting decorations and the cellos grumble rustically below. The opening strain returns, again briefly; but the serenade melody dominates this movement rather than the opening dance. In the coda, Berlioz poses an interesting technical problem by combining three ideas at two tempos. The dance rhythm is carried at its regular speed by the orchestral violas as the soloist plays the serenade melody and the high woodwinds take the Harold theme in long-held notes in a wind-down that's beautiful and charming.

Filled with explosive contrasts and summing up the work excitingly, the subtitle of the finale is "The brigand's orgies. Reminiscences of the preceding scenes." Here, Berlioz imitates the finale of Beethoven's Ninth by recalling melodies from earlier in the work and having the new material reject them before taking over. It opens with a crash, followed by the leaping dance theme that will carry the movement to its climactic peaks and wild ending. A sharply accented three-note motto gives the theme its thrust and is repeated often. But almost before it has begun, there's a pause, and an abbreviated version of the opening fugato and the Harold theme are heard. The leaping dance breaks through, pausing for a moment to recall the pilgrim's march of the second movement. Another choreographic outburst is interrupted momentarily by the mountaineer's serenade of the third movement, here taken by the solo viola. Another eruption, this interrupted by the first movement's suave pendant theme; then one more debate between the wild dance and a dreamy iteration of the Harold theme. Berlioz's use of Beethoven's example is so clearly in tribute that it can't be called plagiarism. And unlike Bruckner—who also copied Beethoven openly and clumsily in the finale of his Symphony No. 5—this is as every bit as good as the model.

At last the dance is allowed to run its wild course, with several enormous and thrilling climaxes for an extension of the theme that reaches toward ecstasy. But shrewdly, Berlioz gives the wild and thunderous material greater impact by allowing many quieter, delicately scored moments to steal in. The composer works in one last thematic surprise as the ecstatic dance is made to scurry in quietly and contrapuntally, followed by a surprising slowdown and diminuendo (reduction of volume) for the last recurrence of the pilgrim's hymn, scored for the solo viola and, in an aural and dramatic inspiration, two violins and a cello playing meditatively from offstage. In the end the dance theme, driven by a new syncopated rhythm, pushes to a tremendous and melodramatic closing.

The Flop: *Symphonie funèbre et triomphale* ("Funereal and Triumphal Symphony")

A big part of the difficulty for this work of 1840 is that it's misnamed and misunderstood. It's really a three-movement suite originally for brass, winds, and percussion composed on commission for two outdoor processions and a memorial service, not a symphonic work like those discussed earlier in this chapter. Hoping the music might have a life in the concert hall, Berlioz later added strings and chorus to the last movement only, but not too surprisingly the additions sound awkward. But though it's little heard today, the *Symphonie funèbre* was a success on July 28, 1840, when it was first performed and other musicians, including the composer's nemesis, François-Antoine Habeneck, spoke of it with admiration: "the bastard has some damned fine ideas . . ." and no less than Richard Wagner claimed that he was "inclined to rank this composition above all Berlioz' other ones . . ."[15] Few today see it that way, but certainly the composer of *Lohengrin* might well have admired its brassy fanfares; and clearly it served as a milestone for Berlioz himself in his revisions and reconceiving of his own Requiem.

Set in three movements, the *Symphonie funèbre* opens with its longest section, a *Marche funèbre* that starts with drum rolls and brass and winds playing a solemn theme that's not unimpressive on its own, followed by a contrasting lyrical idea for winds. The march lasts for nearly twenty minutes though. If it sounds bombastic, that's because it had to be; if the four-square phrasing bothers you, keep in mind that it was written for musicians performing as they marched, for whom the composer's typical rhythmic subtleties would have been confusing and unwelcome.

A lyrical trombone solo dominates the second-movement *Oraison funèbre*—the first word means "prayer." If you like the trombone used this way, the movement may speak to you; or it may not. The finale, titled *Apothéose*, moves at a quicker tempo and also carries the odd addition of strings and chorus singing a prayer of praise, which seem to come from nowhere after the two long sections without them. The composer builds to a big climax at the end on a key change that's reasonably impressive.

It may be fair to credit Berlioz for good instrumental writing here and there and for devising a form where the second and third movements balance the first in length. But listeners who love the composer for his fleet-footedness and unpredictability will probably find the *Symphonie funèbre* dreary and unwieldy. Be that as it may, it's important to keep in mind that it was written for a memorial service in an age and for an aesthetic that genuinely appreciated pompous public funeral marches.

The Concert Overtures

All six works in this chapter are good examples of the composer's style at its most energetic. Two, *Le Carnaval romain* ("The Roman Carnival") and *Le Corsaire* ("The Corsair"), are popular with audiences for their brilliance and respected by musicians for their displays of Berlioz's technical mastery. As we'll see, though, at least three of the others are great fun to hear and deserve wider appreciation.

Most of the six concert overtures began life as preludes to operas that were either abandoned or absorbed into other works. As noted, *Le Carnaval romain* has always been one of Berlioz's most popular orchestral showpieces. An adaptation of material from *Benvenuto Cellini*, it's also widely regarded as the greatest of the six, with *Corsaire* a close second. The overtures to his operas *Benvenuto Cellini* and *Béatrice et Bénédict* are discussed with the works themselves. Both overtures are great and performed by themselves; *Les Troyens* opens without an overture. Berlioz's concert overtures mostly follow a two-part pattern: after a short, arresting opening, there's an extended, lyrical slow section, then an exciting, quick-tempo second part.

Great operatic overtures, particularly the best by Mozart, Rossini, Wagner, and Verdi, form an extraordinary category, setting the stage for the music-dramas they introduce with many presenting musical ideas that are enlarged over the course of the operas. Its cousin the concert overture, also called a dramatic overture, is a stand-alone version, taking its title from a stage play but without an opera to follow. Berlioz's concert overtures are parades of themes, which are then put into musical debate or conflict to summarize each drama in its progress.

Most concert overtures were based on models by Beethoven, the *Egmont* and *Coriolanus*, as well as the three titled *Leonora*. The latter were all written as overtures for *Fidelio*, Beethoven's only opera. Of a length and power that overwhelmed the stage drama, these were shelved, though they stand on their own and are remain favorite listening, especially the *Leonora* No. 3. They spawned countless offspring by Mendelssohn, Weber, Brahms, Dvořák, and others. Interestingly, Berlioz conceived the two earliest of his (*Waverley* and *Franc-Juges*) before hearing Beethoven's music, so they reflect other influences, mostly that of now-forgotten French composers.[16] And as we'll see, *Francs-Juges* is a work of enormous personality that's great fun to hear.

Francs-juges translates literally as "free judges," but the title of the opera is translated as "The Judges of the Secret Court,"[17] and that's how Berlioz and his contemporaries of 1826, when he wrote it, understood its meaning. Published seven years later and revised over that period, the *Grande Ouverture des Francs-Juges* is a substantial work that had a life as a concert piece during the composer's lifetime but sank into obscurity. The overture opens quietly, with an idea that combines mystery and pathos, followed by a long, blustering idea for the lower woodwinds and brass that portrays "the opera's despotic ruler,"[18] but in any case, a villain. Pleading flutes and oboes interspersed among the blasts sound like the musical depiction of someone begging for mercy. Things quiet down for a long, temporizing passage with a genuinely Berliozian idea, as timpani pulse off the beat under a long crescendo. A very quick, high-energy theme for the violins depicts conflict and mystery; it's followed by another memorable, contrasting major-key idea over a limping accompaniment that's easily remembered and must have been the chief melody of a crucial aria. There's more conflict among contrasting ideas, such as a long, falling phrase for the flutes and clarinets that are thrown against a scurrying string figure; again, the composer shows his skill at writing for percussion with a carefully conceived dialogue for timpani and the bass drum. The major-key aria melody is heard again, then the high-energy theme for violins interspersed with more weeping for the woodwinds. Berlioz builds to a big, major-key climax for the aria tune and a closing phrase for which he has shrewdly held back a few rhythmic and harmonic surprises.

The Concert Overtures

The overture to *Les Francs-Juges* may not be the greatest piece of music ever written, or even out of Berlioz's top drawer. But it's consistently engrossing and fun to hear, with its quirks and peculiarities adding to its appeal. A recording by the mighty Chicago Symphony Orchestra under Georg Solti makes a fine case for it.

The *Grande Overture de Waverley* is based on a work by Sir Walter Scott, whose novels were enormously popular in the first half of the nineteenth century and used as the plots of several operas. Mostly set in Scotland, which to cynical urban audiences symbolized a supposedly unspoiled edge of Europe, they're full of what were perceived as Highland atmosphere. Donizetti's *Lucia di Lammermoor* is by far the most famous of these; Rossini's *La Donna del Lago*—The Lady of the Lake—is less known but also good. Berlioz's overture to *Waverley* fits this mold. It was probably composed in 1827 but was not published until 1839, and thanks to its longer gestation, is more polished than *Francs-Juges*.

Set in two broad halves, the overture's first part moves at slow and moderate tempos. *Waverley* opens with a hesitating phrase for oboes, then a falling figure for the strings as the French horns comment. No real melody appears for the first two minutes of this ten-minute work. That's relieved by the appearance of a gloriously open tune for the cellos set against a rocking accompaniment to which the woodwinds and French horns add rich canonic imitation; again, Berlioz introduces the timpani as a subtle and unexpectedly quiet underpinning. The quick-tempo second half opens with a brisk rising figure for the violins that contains a bit of a Scottish snap, then moves on to a more triumphant phrase for the full orchestra. But that's followed by a much more peculiar (but characterful) pecking phrase for the woodwinds. The violins then decorate the pecking phrase in a wildly busy version. Berlioz shuffles the rising and pecking phrases in close alternation as he builds to a big climax.

Berlioz composed the *Grande Ouverture du Roi Lear, Tragédie de Shakespeare* (presumably the title doesn't need translation) in Nice in 1831. Enraged at his then-girlfriend Camille Moke, he poured fury into this impressionistic but formally disciplined overture. How well it represents the characters and plot of *King Lear* has been debated from the start, but what matters ultimately is whether it works musically, and that, too, is up for debate. The composer himself, a tough self-critic who had not heard it for years, was thrilled by an 1863 performance.[19] The British musicologist D. F. Tovey loved *Roi Lear*, schizophrenically taking it apart as un-Shakespearean but praising it musically from start to finish. Tovey's article also mentions the admiration for this overture of the composer Richard Strauss, a major endorsement by any standard.[20] Later biographers and commentators are mixed, with David Cairns, for example, defending it against Tovey's critiques,[21] while D. Kern Holoman takes a cooler view: "like the *Francs-Juges* overture and *Waverley*, [it is] more interesting as a stage in his maturation than as a compositional success."[22] For some, while the *Roi Lear* overture may be more skillfully wrought than the other two, it's somehow less effective and interesting.

The angry falling theme for the double basses alone that opens the work in a stately tempo clearly delineates the imperious old king. It's also one of the earliest and most successful adaptations of the same basic idea taken from the finale of Beethoven's Symphony No. 9, where the basses interrupt while actually holding together other themes as they're introduced. Also impressive, if less clearly identifiable as a character or incident, is a long, rapturous tune for the oboe that's of great beauty. It's accompanied and decorated as it progresses by ever-richer accompaniments, then taken up by other instrumental sections, with the French horns giving it the most opulent treatment. The imperious theme comes back, accompanied by drum rolls and blasts from the heavy brass. The quick second half opens with a fiercely energetic theme for the strings that, again, is impossible to apply with specificity to the play. The oboe leads with a contrasting lyrical idea, and a number of its developmental offspring suggest spoken dialogues. The double basses come back at the quick tempo in a conflict-laden passage. A final, furious iteration of that double-bass theme is broken by chords for the brass, as the composer ends with a melodramatic coda.

Written in Italy in 1831, the *Intrata di Rob-Roy MacGregor*, "a bright work brimming with rhythmic and melodic invention,"[23] is rarely performed and little known but really excellent and ripe for revival. Based on another novel by Sir Walter Scott, this substantial composition has much in the way of Highland affect as well as the main theme of *Harold en Italie*, lovingly developed and here sounding Scottish. The overture was poorly received at its only performance in Berlioz's lifetime in Paris, and the discouraged composer burned one score; happily, another survived. Or, as Tovey wrote: "In Berlioz's vocabulary 'burnt' means carefully preserved . . . The Overture to *Rob-Roy* turned up early in this [the twentieth] century, and proved to be quite a presentable and engaging work."[24] You'll be astonished by how immediately appealing *Rob-Roy* is.

Horn calls set against pizzicato strings in a dance rhythm dominate the opening section of this work, which is set in three parts, with opening material recurring as the third section (ABA) rather than the usual binary pattern. A mock-stern passage for lower winds and strings that's decorated by chattering flutes follows. Soon, though, what would become one of the *Harold* themes appears, here on the English horn, followed by a stirring iteration of the Scottish dance theme for the full orchestra. Prepare to be startled by the ensuing slowdown and the appearance of harps and the main theme of *Harold en Italie*, here laid forth convincingly by the English horn (not the viola) and harp in intimate dialogue. Soon the orchestra joins with the same rapturous commentary as in *Harold*, which was begun shortly after the abandonment of *Rob-Roy*. The more vigorous Scottish tunes come back again to round out the ABA form, and there's an exciting coda filled with Scottish themes, here made more interesting by the composer's unconventional harmonic underpinnings.

If the number of recorded versions is the measurement, then *Le Carnaval romain*—The Roman Carnival, Track 2—with its descriptive subtitle *ouverture caractéristique*, takes second place in popularity to the *Symphonie fantastique* in Berlioz's oeuvre. And rightly so: this brilliant work is endlessly appealing, displaying the mature composer's style at its most fully developed, impeccable in form and approaching perfection. Composed between 1843 and 1844, it's also a hybrid of very old themes, including one from the *Messe solennelle* of 1824 here transformed from sacred to secular, where it seems to fit better. It's also a take-off on the scenario of *Benvenuto Cellini* of 1838, with the excitement of a Roman carnival and a love duet played out in a highly condensed orchestral form. The most concise of the overtures, these breathtaking eight minutes represent one of Berlioz's greatest works and one of the gems of the concert overture repertory.

It is so fast moving that a prose description is something of a trap. The glittering, sometimes riotous orchestration must be heard to believed; but when you listen, attend to the dashing opening phrase followed by giggling stings and stuttering woodwinds that occupy fifteen seconds, then the calm passage with a long, irregular melody for the English horn that's taken from the *Cellini* love duet—another of the master's great tunes—here rendered with a rare balance of passion and poise. After that, though, things take off at wild speed and thematic density, sometimes laid out in full phrases but often in fragments. A dance called a saltarello that first scampers then explodes is the main thematic material for the fast section; this, remarkably, began life in the 1824 *Messe* before migrating to *Benvenuto Cellini*, then here. Continual jolts of rhythm and harmony to the very end keep *Le Carnaval romain* surprising and fresh.

The first performance of the *Ouverture du Corsaire* was in 1845, though the history of its composition isn't fully known.[25] The title refers to the romantic pirate created by Lord Byron whose work inspired *Harold en Italie*. It is, like *Le Carnaval romain*, one of the great dramatic overtures. *Corsaire* is bit broader and more comprehensible in its structure, with longer thematic statements, though through much of this short and intense work you have to hold on for dear life. *Corsaire* opens with a short, swaggering phrase followed by the presentation of a gorgeous, richly harmonized slow melody. Playfully exchanged phrases for the woodwinds and strings lead to a return of the quick tempo of the opening, with ideas tossed around in an exchange that's always cheerful. These consist of long phrases that are also appealingly irregular in the composer's best manner. The opening passage is recapitulated, and a vigorous, unmistakably masculine main theme builds to an accelerating climax for the full orchestra. Be sure to enjoy the trademarked Berliozian harmonic shocks built into the cadences toward the end.

Berlioz the Shakespearean

The Tragedy: *Roméo et Juliette*

Berlioz composed this daring symphony in 1839, revising it again in 1847 and 1857. Shakespeare is its direct inspiration; the mold-breaking Beethoven of the Symphony No. 9 is just as significant an influence. As one commentator notes: "It is the work that makes sense not just of [Berlioz's] symphonies, but of his entire canon—that shows him most clearly as both a symphonist in search of the theater and a dramatist most comfortable with the language of music."[26]

Yet *Roméo et Juliette* "remains one of his least performed works, a favourite more of musicians than of the public."[27] This observation is borne out by the thirty-three performances of this ninety-minute symphony, noble yet challenging, on the ArkivMusic website, with most also available on Spotify. Like many other musical masterworks, *Roméo et Juliette* demands effort and time of the listener. If you've never heard it, then the third movement Love Scene (Track 3) and the fourth movement scherzo will probably appeal to you first. But to hear them out of context keeps you from grasping their role in the composer's carefully planned structure, and ignores its grand scale. Of course, the Love Scene is a long, lyrical slow movement; the scherzo is also a stunning example of its type. Attempts to make everything follow a conventional symphonic structure are pointless in the face of the originality of the composer's conception and the brilliance of his execution.

Berlioz's subtitle for *Roméo et Juliette* is *Symphonie dramatique*. In addition to the orchestra, this seven-movement symphony features three soloists and a chorus, acting mostly as the angry and mournful voices of the feuding families of the play, in the first, second, fifth, sixth, and seventh movements. The orchestra alone performs movements three and four. The three soloists are a bass-baritone, who sings what most resembles an operatic role, Père Laurence, Friar Laurence in Shakespeare; a contralto and tenor each sing one aria in the first movement.

The title characters are not sung; the orchestra covers the sense of their words and emotions. Berlioz wisely decided that not only were their words were too passionate for setting, but settings of passionate words in love duets were already too common, explaining in his foreword,

> since duets of this nature have been handled vocally a thousand times by the greatest masters, it was wise as well as unusual to attempt another means of expression. It is also because the very sublimity of this love made its depiction so dangerous for the musician that he had to give his imagination a latitude that the positive sense of the sung words would not have given him, resorting instead to instrumental language, which is richer, more varied, less precise, and by its very indefiniteness incomparably more powerful in such a case.[28]

Although an excellent writer, Berlioz in 1839 still lacked the confidence to create the text himself. He asked the writer and translator Émile Deschamps for help, giving this important if not exactly irreplaceable collaborator one breezy mention in his autobiography.[29] Certainly the patronage and friendship of the string virtuoso Niccolò Paganini, who, after finally hearing *Harold en Italie*, gave Berlioz 20,000 francs for an unspecified composition of Berlioz's choosing, was of greater import. Paganini freed Berlioz to work and follow his instincts. Paganini gets the composer's profuse thanks in the *Memoirs*, as well as the dedication of *Roméo et Juliette*.

Fights. Tumult. Intervention of the Prince

Berlioz breaks from standard symphonic form in the opening movement, an assortment of parts that may at first seem random. Here, he tells explicitly in words what the work is about, and implicitly in music as well, previewing some of its thematic material.

Its opening phrases instantly capture the aggression between the families, and the listener's attention too. Starting in the violas and laden with spiky trills, Berlioz's tempo and expression mark is *allegro fugato*, meaning "quick and in a fuguelike manner," but the counterpoint is loose and soon interrupted by a rising phrase in the brass and powerful syncopated chords that break the momentum of the fight. More regularly placed chords for the brass signal the arrival of the Prince and his imperious proclamation, again for the heavy brass, mostly halting the battle. This is depicted in fragments of the fugato that flicker along the sidelines even after the most emphatic of the Prince's thunderings, again taking over and ending this marvelous prelude quietly, while demonstrating musically that the Capulet-Montague feud is still far from over.

Three sections that follow continue to set the scene. A sweep on the harp sets a bardic tone, as the contralto narrator and chorus take up Berlioz's summary of Shakespeare's opening lines: D'anciennes haines endormies—Of old sleeping hatreds. Taken in the play by a spoken chorus, here they are sung in free and noble recitative-like phrases. The tone changes as Roméo is described longingly watching Juliette at a ball in the Capulets' palace. The strutting dance theme that's fully developed in the second movement bursts in, but quickly dies down. Although Wagner didn't begin *Tristan und Isolde* for another eighteen years, Berlioz writes a huge, sighing phrase that foreshadows *Tristan* in melodic profile and intensity as Roméo is described finding Juliette on her balcony, confessing her love of him to the night. This is the main theme of the third movement Love Scene.

The next section has the unusual title *Strophes*. These are two long verses (Premiers transportes—First raptures) in praise of love and of Shakespeare. Sung by the contralto, the lines are accompanied throughout by a flowing harp, joined in the second verse by a passionate commentary for the cellos. Although they seem static after the impetus of opening sections, their tone, lyrical and reflective rather than hectic, also continues the boldness of the preceding passages for chorus. They make greater sense each time you listen.

The opening movement is rounded out with an exchange between the chorus and the tenor soloist, introducing la Reine Mab—Queen Mab—a deluding fairy mentioned by Romeo's friend Mercutio in the first act of the play. As we'll see, the composer expands the role of the fairy music exponentially in the scherzo that is the fourth movement of *Roméo et Juliette*. Here titled Scherzetto (little scherzo), the composer lightens textures and speeds up considerably, giving a taste of thematic material with little hint of the mind-boggling dimensions of the fully developed scherzo. The movement ends with the chorus gloomily forecasting the tragic ending.

Roméo alone. Sadness. Concert and ball. Great festivities at the Capulets' palace.

Berlioz's Roméo alone through the great festivities at the Capulets' forms the second movement of *Roméo et Juliette*. This long, musically diverse section reflects all of the contrasts described in the composer's layout, but it's also a tightly woven fabric of recurring thematic material with steady development toward a climactic ending, manifested in thickening textures, greater volume, and accelerating tempos.

Like the surging love theme in part 1, several of Berlioz's ideas here clearly made a big impression on Wagner. This is true of the long, floating, almost rhythm-free melody that opens this section, which seems to anticipate specific passages in both *Tristan und Isolde* and *Parsifal*. Berlioz's hovering tune depicts Roméo's solitude as he watches the Capulets' party, then slips inside. The composer keeps the theme mostly unsupported for a daring length. Finally giving voice to Roméo's sadness, another, this one sweetly melancholy, is given to the oboe over a steadily flowing accompaniment in the strings. It's extended in the strings and high winds over more insistent, pulsing accompaniments. Bits of the swaggering dance we heard a bit of in part 1 steal in at low volume, with the tambourine giving gentle but distinct emphasis. The oboe spins out its long melody again, with the tambourine now joining in an irresistible call to the dance.

This new section contrasts as vividly as it might with the preceding. In an introductory passage, the composer picks up the tempo in preparation for the main theme, which is the swaggering dance sampled in the first movement and in an undertone in the introductory section here. Now Berlioz unrolls it in full splendor, initially with a stateliness that grows frantic as it progresses.

Somehow Berlioz works in the melancholy theme representing Roméo's sadness from the previous section, now roared out in long notes by the French horns; the composer proudly notes in the score his achievement of *Réunion des deux Thèmes*, the reunion of the two themes, which actually seems overdone. But as the dance approaches its wildest climax, the uproar is quieted to let the oboe play the melancholy theme slowly again. Then the dance theme is allowed to reach the anticipated thunderous ending, reminiscent of the closing pages of *Harold en Italie*. As we've seen and will again, one of this composer's skills is to set boundaries that sound unsurpassable, be it in speed, volume, rhythmic compression, energy, or emotional extravagance, then knock that boundary down.

The third movement Scène d'amour—Love scene—stands at the center of the work; it's also its heart and soul, and the composer's favorite child among his many creations. "If you ask me which of my works I prefer," wrote Berlioz in 1858, "my answer is that of most artists: the love scene in 'Romeo and Juliet.'"[30]

Here's where the composer's free approach to Shakespeare really pays off. Listeners will surely make out Romeo's ardent declarations in the masculine tones of the violas, cellos, and horns; Juliet's replies can be heard in the flutes; the knocking of Juliet's maid can be imagined in certain quick, rapping figures. But the key to Berlioz's triumph is that they are imagined by the listener rather than heard in the literal, trite words of a translated text. (In his Nocturne in D-flat Major, Op. 27, No. 2, Chopin takes a similar approach, where two lovers' voices are artfully imitated on the piano, fiery oaths and all.)

In keeping with the spacious proportions of *Roméo et Juliette*, Berlioz precedes the Love Scene proper with a mood-setting number for a chorus of tiring but still excited revelers leaving the Capulets' party. They call to each other tipsily in lowering volume and rhythmically flexible phrases that capture their dispersion into the streets.

The Love Scene itself begins with pulsating figures in the strings beneath sighs from the English horn and clarinets. Roméo's theme, interspersed with Juliette's replies, appears in the violas and French horns. The composer allows this great, arching tune—admired by Wagner as "the melody of the nineteenth century"[31]—an expanding role, extending its phrasing over the course of the scene. Knocking interruptions, handled with comic verve, change the tone and pacing, as does a recitative-like passage for the cellos, the masculine tone of which clearly represent Roméo's voice, with the high woodwinds' reply as Juliette. A bit later, the duet moves fluidly again as the rarely paired flute and English horn, also perhaps suggesting the lovers' voices, engage in a long dialogue over a dense, unconventional accompaniment for the strings. Again, the composer steers back to his glorious arc of a melody. Even at its most rich and dense, his scoring is transparent, as the essential clarity of his style purifies the music. Another gorgeous passage that depicts a passion too strong for words features panting, syncopated, rising chords for the woodwinds that move to an unexpected harmony, accompanied by pulsating figuration in the strings. After more dialogue-like moments the melody is allowed one more glorious eruption, as this great love-duet without singers moves in gentle instrumental exchanges, but without fuss, to a quiet conclusion.

Queen Mab is the fairy described and debated by Romeo and his friend Mercutio in act 1, scene 4 of the play. Romeo points out that dreams often reveal truth, setting Mercutio, who disagrees, off in a comical, image-laden tirade against Mab, their supposed instigator. Sensing the need for a lighter interlude in this long, serious work, Berlioz finds his opportunity in Mercutio's rant. The resulting scherzo, its fourth movement, is one of the greatest in the repertory. There are different types of scherzo in music, though, with some serious examples by Beethoven and Chopin. Others, like la Reine Mab, are of an elfin nature; some, combining the demonic and the playful, form a third category in between. Most famous among the elfin type are Mendelssohn's, from his *Incidental Music to* A Midsummer Night's Dream, and Weber's *Oberon*, both of which surely influenced Berlioz.

But *Reine Mab* tops the other fairy music in its ambitions and execution. Absolutely consistent in tone and texture, it's also the most exquisitely orchestrated section in *Roméo et Juliette* and a working lesson in orchestration. It moves at a remarkable clip as well. A road map may help, but keep in mind that there's nothing that flies by quite like this. The composer stuffs so much into its performing time of seven or eight minutes that repeated listening is needed just to get your bearings; and more beauties reveal themselves as you come to know it.

Berlioz's tempo is prestissimo—very quick—which he holds for two-thirds of the movement. The first half-minute or so consists of fragments of the scampering principal theme alternating with bumps, burps, stutters, hiccups, trills, and sustained chords for the high winds that seem long only in this breakneck context. Although the material it's made from is unquestionably witty, the effect of Queen Mab is breathtaking rather than funny. The main theme has a symmetrical phrasing as it rises, then falls. It's repeated, with the initial statement and repeat taking less than thirty seconds. An expansion of the material includes a lilting melodic fragment for flute and oboe and a slithering chromatic fall in the strings. There are more hiccups in rhythm than you can count, and Berlioz keeps the dynamics mostly to *pianissimo*—very soft. Increases in volume are moderate and done almost before they register on the ear.

Four trills for the violins lead the (slightly) slower middle section. Here the flute and English horn trade rising and lengthening phrases of a more mysterious cast as the harps join in and the violins add long notes in a weird, whistling tone called harmonics. Once the mysterious tune is fully unfurled we realize it's the principal theme, stretched out into distorted, dreamlike phrasing. The violas also sputter it out below in a more recognizable pattern. The prestissimo tempo returns along with the main theme, also opening a marvelous passage for four French horns. These call to one another softly in a galloping motif, as though from great distances. Deeper-pitched instruments, including bassoons and timpani, join, leading to two galloping climaxes for the full orchestra, both of which are over in an instant. Also joining in are antique cymbals, a rarely heard percussion instrument with a delicate, ringing tone. The main theme scatters quietly across the full orchestra;

some almost-serious, long-held chords for the strings lead to an amusing exchange among harps, strings, winds, and the antique cymbals. There's a final iteration of the theme as a rising scale sweeps everything away.

With its lavish treatment of minimal thematic material, *La Reine Mab* is, paradoxically, a marvel of restraint. Some complain of a lack of polish in Berlioz's style, but this is the work of a master in full control of his ideas and technique. Both Debussy and Ravel seem to have learned much from this movement. Debussy's ballet *Jeux*—Games—shares its textural density and kaleidoscopic mobility. Among other similarities, Ravel's *Daphnis et Chloé*, also a ballet, features elaborate scoring for the percussion, which includes finger cymbals that sound much like the antique ones called for here.

The fifth movement was created from a scene that's not in the original but instead derived from Berlioz's corrupt, translated version of the play[32] the Convoi funèbre de Juliette—Funeral procession of Juliette. No matter: its mournful character sets the mood for the drama's tragic outcome, and it's carefully planned and beautifully executed. The composer's design begins with a slow, quiet fugue for the orchestra, against which a large chorus intones a gloomy phrase on one note: E. Midway through, the pattern switches, as the chorus takes up counterpoint and the orchestra picks up the monotonous material, though less rigidly. There's also an archlike structure as the movement begins and ends in thin textures, reaching greater density toward the middle.

The cellos give out the desolate fugue subject, with the chorus chanting its phrase, Jetez des fleurs pour la vierge expirée—Cast flowers for the late virgin. The instrumental commentary is marked by falling figures that seem to sigh and weep. But just when monotony threatens, the composer shrewdly changes the textures. He tightens the rhythm, as violas and cellos move into pizzicato triplets, and shifts the harmony consolingly. (This passage is strikingly prescient of Mahler.) The consolatory passage is brief, as the darker tonality, weeping figures, and thick counterpoint take over again.

That gloom is relieved, however, by two changes, both achieved quietly, both quietly startling. Unaccompanied by the orchestra, the chorus takes up the fugue subject, in the relative major (E major) of the tonality that has dominated. The orchestra, led by the violins, repeats a rhythmic figure over and over. Berlioz brings back the idea prefiguring Mahler in the major key, accompanied by a flowing figuration in the flutes and clarinets. He also pares the orchestral textures as the fugue subject becomes the main focus again. But as the violins and flutes pulse through bar after bar of bare-sounding Es, the harmony beneath begins to grind gently but disturbingly against what our ears have grown comfortable with. The composer is preparing us for the sixth movement, consisting of three short scenes that begin in high drama and end tragically.

That sixth movement of *Roméo et Juliette* sets the "tomb scene" (act 5, scene 4) of the play. The most openly programmatic and pictorial part of the work is strong stuff, leaving little doubt as to what it's depicting. Again, listeners who are familiar with *Romeo and Juliet* need to keep in mind that Berlioz was working from a corrupt translation of the play. In Shakespeare, Romeo dies before Juliet wakes and she exchanges only a few lines with Friar Laurence before stabbing herself. Thus, the frantic instrumental dialogues between the two imagined by the composer have no parallel in the play.

Opening with a jolting passage for the full orchestra, Berlioz avoids a clear beat that might let us get our bearings; this depicts Roméo's desperation on arriving at the Capulets' tomb. In the solemn, widely spaced chords for the brass, winds, and strings we hear his entry to the tomb and look at its dreadful contents. His long, grieving address to the various dead Capulets (and the apparently dead Juliet) is the burden of the beautiful, grief-stricken Invocation. Over limping figuration in the lower strings, a long-limbed but irregular melody for the unusual but masculine combination of English horn, bassoons, and French horn rises and falls. The entry of trombones deepens the gloom as does broken, chromatic shuddering in the cellos and double basses. The composer thins the orchestral texture as the hero drinks poison; this passage also clearly set an example for Wagner, who parallels it closely in act 1 of *Tristan und Isolde* when his lovers drink their potion.

As Juliette wakes from her drugged sleep, we hear fragments of one of her themes from the Love Scene. The frantic orchestral outburst as she and Roméo embrace is also more poignant for being laden with references to the Love Scene, but soon interrupted by dizzy figures picturing Roméo's seizure and death. Juliette's suicide is also vividly shown by a leaping figure as she stabs herself followed by a slowly falling line for the oboe as her life departs.

Soloists and chorus return for the cantata-like seventh movement. First comes a fast-moving passage in which Veronans express their horror on finding the bodies of the hero and heroine, and a recitative for Père Laurence. Opening with blasts from the brass, the Capulets express outrage at finding the tomb violated by Roméo. But perhaps the finest moment comes when the chorus realizes that both have just died and the volume drops from loud to a softly murmured Morts tous les deux, et leur sang fume encore—Both dead and their blood still fresh. Laurence narrates the history of their secret love and wedding and, to an ever-tightening accompaniment led by a falling figure for the violins, the events that led to their catastrophic end.

The final sections of *Roméo et Juliette* are packed with texts of shifting tone, to which Berlioz is fully alert. The beginning of the aria of Père Laurence (Pauvres enfants que je pleure—Poor children for whom I weep) is warm and soothing, with a noble melody worthy of Beethoven that also captures his regret at the disastrous outcome of all good intentions, including his own. But once Laurence asks the Montagues and Capulets, represented by the chorus, to see their feud as the root of the catastrophe, the musical setting shifts to a chastising tone and faster tempo. From here to the end, he assumes a new role as the voice of God, first angry, then commanding, and finally consoling as the clans finally swear to end their feud. Before that, though, the battle is resumed in the cemetery. Berlioz returns to the aggressive opening phrases of the symphony, now rendered even more furious by interjections of the chorus.

Laurence interrupts them thunderously, showing the lovers who are also their beloved heirs dead at their feet: Silence, malheureux! Pouvez-vous sans remors devant un tel amour, étaler tant de haine? (Quiet, you unfortunates! Are you without remorse before such a love, [still] spreading so much hate?) Now in tones of anger tinged with sorrow, Laurence calls on God to enlighten the souls of these men, who cannot let go of their hatred. Known in French and English as the Invocation, this impressive passage (Grand Dieu, qui voit au fond de l'âme—God, who sees to the depths of the soul) is reminiscent of an operatic oath, and sets the tone for the closing number which follows. Over a throbbing accompaniment, Laurence's phrases are punctuated by a rising figure for the bassoons and low strings. The rising intensity of his manner finally catches the attention of the feuding families, here voiced by the chorus. The composer depicts their transformation in a fairly standard musical shift from the prevailing minor key to its relative major, a moment that's effectively underlined by a soothing line for the cellos.

Roméo et Juliette ends with a real oath, Jurez, donc—Swear, then—between the Montagues and Capulets, led and blessed by Père Laurence. Set in the unusual, long-limbed 9/8 meter he loved, Berlioz initially seems to adopt a throbbing accompaniment like that in the previous number. But soon, richly detailed commentary from the orchestra, including trills in the cellos and double basses and falling figures for the higher strings, show this to be a movement of far greater range and power. Sophisticated harmonic shifts, exciting rhythmic contractions, and orchestral lightning and thunder make what could have been an exercise in bombast into an ending that's stirring and genuinely moving. Mahler demonstrated some of what he learned from *Roméo et Juliette* in the choral finale of his Symphony No. 2, the "Resurrection."

The Comedy: *Béatrice et Bénédict*

Based on *Much Ado About Nothing*, this opera is Berlioz's last major work and a formidable romantic comedy. Although flawed, *Béatrice et Bénédict* is a minor masterpiece that deserves more exposure and wider appreciation. Its chief complication and drawback are the frequent interruptions for long passages of spoken dialogue. These are often cut as much as they may be while maintaining the intelligibility of the slim but busy plot, as in the 1978 recording led by Colin Davis. Ultimately, however, the work is more comprehensible with the dialogue, and complete performances, such as the 1992 recording conducted by John Nelson, hold together structurally and make better dramatic sense. In the Nelson-led performance, actors, not the singers, perform the spoken parts precluding the difficulties vocalists seem to experience with spoken scripts, while also running up the cost of producing *Béatrice* with two performers (one singer, one actor) on the payroll for the six principal roles. (This approach wouldn't work at all in a staged production.) Another intelligent solution can be heard in the star-studded 1982 recording under Daniel Barenboim, where the dialogues are condensed into summaries read by a narrator. In any case, there's no single or easy way to deal with this aspect of the opera.

All these difficulties hold *Béatrice et Bénédict* to a cult favorite status, a shame, because its indisputable strengths include marvelous character depiction and great music with the master's orchestration at its lightest and most highly evolved. It's cleverly structured, genuinely funny at times, and never dull, a mosaic of gorgeous individual numbers.

Berlioz had been thinking of writing an opera based on *Much Ado* since 1833,[33] and a commission from a small opera house in Baden, Germany, in 1860 finally got the project going. The composer wrote the libretto himself, cutting one of the main (for many *the* main) story lines, leaving a very light plot where lovers who feign dislike but are actually attracted to each other wind up betrothed after various but essentially minor tribulations. As every commentator points out, the crux of Shakespeare's play is a plot against the virtue of Hero, who, with Beatrice in both play and opera, are the principal female characters. What's left is lots of business for everyone except the title characters to bring them together, while those two discover themselves and ultimately confess their attraction for each other. Berlioz cut Dogberry and Verges, two of Shakespeare's comic characters, replacing them with the pedantic music master of his own invention, Maestro Somarone, who is extraneous to the plot but appears in both acts.

Because it's Berlioz's last opera and a comedy based on Shakespeare, *Béatrice et Bénédict* gets compared unfavorably to Verdi's *Falstaff*. And certainly, it's the lesser of the two, lacking the power, momentum, and tight internal organization of Verdi's masterwork. What Berlioz composed is an opera of individual elements, relatively modest in scope, that's not quite perfectly assembled or balanced, with the hour-long first act twenty minutes longer than the second. There are extraneous characters, such as Somarone, and numbers that fail to advance the story. But with arias, ensembles, choruses, and instrumental interludes that are smaller in scale, the aging Berlioz, like an even older Verdi, finds wisdom about the human condition, which he expresses with wit and great beauty throughout. Each of the individual bits that make up the score of *Béatrice* is beautifully conceived and orchestrated with the composer's skill at its peak. Even a casual listening reveals its quality.

The work opens with a substantial overture that's another concert favorite. It's a skillful potpourri of thematic material from the opera. It differs from Berlioz's other overtures by opening directly and without flourish with the theme of the playful, ironic duet for the reluctant lovers that ends the opera. There's a scampering motif that reappears several times and unifies the overture, but five or six other tunes from the opera also appear. The whole is seamless, lively, and orchestrated with the composer's customary skill and even more than his typical refinement. Act 1 opens with a cheerful chorus of Sicilians welcoming Don Pedro, the Sicilian general, and his soldiers, including Bénédict and Claudio, back from a victory over the infidel Moors. Some plot-advancing dialogue follows in which we learn of the love of Hero (daughter of Leonato, governor of Sicily) and Claudio. A swift-moving second choral movement, La More est en fuite—The Moor is in flight—features some tantalizing oscillations of harmony. A sicilienne—a lilting tarantella-like dance—makes the first of two appearances in the opera. This brief choreographic interlude is fine-boned and nearly weightless.

With Hero's opening aria, Je vais le voir—I shall see him (referring to Claudio)—a tone of Beethovenian nobility takes over. Berlioz's woodwind writing, with flute and oboe delicately punctuating the singer's line, is reminiscent of Mozart as well. The passionate, quick-tempo section that follows, Il me revient fidèle—Faithful he returns to me—also has a directness and symmetry reminiscent of its classical-era models, but Berlioz inserts some expressive harmonic shifts that sound remarkably fresh. Hero ends the aria with a bright and spectacular cadenza.

Claudio and Hero are reunited, after which the title characters taunt each other in the duet Comment le dédain, pourrait-il mourir?—Is it possible disdain should die?—a fast-moving comic dialogue in which the composer manages the debate between Béatrice and Bénédict primarily with changes in tempo. Sustaining a comic tone within an essentially serious operatic style is not easy, but Berlioz, in the select company of Mozart, Donizetti, and Verdi, does it here. Now the men—Bénédict, Claudio, and Don Pedro—take the stage in a fast-moving, even more brilliant trio: Me marier? Dieu me pardonne?—I marry? God save me! Set in six tightly interwoven sections, Bénédict rails against women, his mother excepted, and curses with exaggerated horror the rest as well as marriage itself. His friends, who are plotting to see him wed Béatrice, chuckle to each other in asides, then reproach Bénédict with mocking extravagance. Berlioz slows the tempo just a bit as the friends call him impious for spurning holy matrimony and ungrateful for his disdain for women, accompanied by a playful rhythmic figure for the oboes, clarinets, and lower strings while the piccolos, flutes, and violins scurry along. There's a seamless change of meter and speed as the debate grows hotter. Perhaps the masterstroke of the ensemble comes with the slowdown to a funereal tempo and tone as Bénédict describes in horror a sign that he swears will never be placed on his house: Ici l'on voit Bénédict, l'homme marié!—Here is Bénédict, married man!—as Don Pedro and Claudio mock him and predict his fall in the same faux-somber tone to the comical gurgling of bassoons.

Somarone ("Donkey"), the pedantic music master who is the composer's invention, is introduced in the next scene to rehearse a chorus he has prepared for the wedding of Hero and Claudio. Berlioz's title for Somarone's choral composition is "Epithalame grotesque," the first word meaning a hymn sung at a wedding. Here Berlioz mocks music that's academically correct but four-square and ugly, as Somarone leads his singers and instrumentalists in a sturdy chorale—Mourez, tendres epoux ("Die, tender pair")—referring to their moment of highest bliss in which the contrapuntal entries are barked out clumsily. This chorus quite obviously echoes the student's "Amen" chorus from the master's *Faust* of fifteen years earlier. Unhappy with his work, Somarone adds a cheerful solo for oboe that's played during the dialogue. The epithalamium is repeated, this time with the oboe accompaniment, which it does improve.

Hiding behind a bush, Bénédict overhears Don Pedro, Claudio, and Leonato say (knowing that he's there and in jest) that Béatrice has fallen in love with him. Since the two are already in love, he expresses his joy in an exuberant aria, Ah, je vais l'aimer—I will love her. Berlioz uses the high winds in a fluttering figure to announce his excitement and perhaps the acceleration of his heart. Note the hair-trigger shift to minor tonality as Bénédict shifts quickly to anger at the idea that he might be dreaming.

The final moments of act 1 are given to a nocturnelike duet between Hero and her maid, Ursule. The scene has no ancestry in *Much Ado* and is purely an invention of the composer's, with a feeble setup: the two women have simply entered the garden as the moon rises. But aside from the overture, Nuit paisible et sereine—Peaceful and serene night—is the best known and loved portion of the opera, and rightly so. Ten minutes of heaven, this ravishing duet displays the composer's lyrical side at its most intense, evolved, and polished. Berlioz's text, laden with references to classical myths, is a vehicle for his musical setting.

A slow dialogue in recitative is punctuated by figures from the clarinets and flutes that depict Hero's blissful sighs. The duet proper opens with the singers taking the melody in close, sweet harmony, with Hero, a soprano, above and Ursule, a mezzo-soprano, below over muted strings with delicate commentary by the oboes, which mimic the chirping of nocturnal insects. The melody starts in a relatively narrow range, but soon bursts out opulently: Qui mêle aux murmures des bois—Who mingles with the murmurs of the woods—as the singers depict the murmuring vocally in overlapping sequences and even sweeter harmonic guise. There's a gentle downward tug of harmony as the text moves to L'ombre de ce grand arbre—The shadow of this great tree—echoing a similar setting from *Le Spectre de la Rose* ("The Ghost of the Rose") from the song cycle *Les Nuits d'été*. After another short recitative in which Hero's tears are revealed to be those of joy, the duet resumes with greater intensity and (if possible) beauty. The two characters leave the stage; the orchestra is left with the last word in a long, lingering postlude. Echoing the duet's opening section, the flutes followed by the clarinets sing its primary melody, soon accompanied by shivering violins, all over plucked notes for the violas and double basses. Berlioz's instrumentation throughout is weightless and flawless, with no percussion or heavy brass instruments; essentially, he uses the orchestra of the high classical era, subtly shaded by the muted strings and the coloristic role he assigns to the oboe.

A slightly expanded version of the sicilienne from act 1 serves as entr'acte and introduction to act 2. Servants preparing for the wedding of Hero and Claudio ask the music master Somarone, who is already drunk, to improvise a drinking song, which he does offstage to the catchy accompaniment of guitars, cornet, trumpet, and a tambourine. Not only is the sonority fresh, the tune he supposedly invents in praise of Sicilian wine effectively suggests an archaic musical style, much as Berlioz did in *Benvenuto Cellini* and *L'Enfance du Christ*. The composer's fondness for rhythmic compression can also be heard in the chorus's interruptions of the ever-drunker music master, who soon finds himself incapable of further improvisation. As you listen you'll hear how polished the composer has made this supposedly rough music.

The musicians exit; told falsely by her friends that Bénédict loves her, Béatrice enters in high agitation. A noble orchestral introduction to her solo scene opens with short, rhythmic outbursts followed by a soaring figure for the violins and flutes. But as she considers the dread she felt the day Bénédict left for war, she confesses to herself that she loves him: Il m'en souvient—It comes back to me. Here, again, one hears the models of Mozart and Beethoven in the nobility of her melodic expression. Agitation returns as she recalls dreaming that he might have been wounded or killed; Berlioz thickens the orchestral texture considerably, adding trumpet calls and stalking figures for the trombones and lower strings; Béatrice calms herself and the orchestra too with the recollection of her relief at waking. The main theme of Il m'en souvient is then recapitulated. The fiery closing section begins as if Béatrice is frightened to admit her love, but soon moves to an easier gait with her acceptance of her new state: Je ne suis pas moi-même—I am no longer myself.

Hero and Ursule now join Béatrice in a trio of musical and dramatic complexity known by Hero's opening words: Je vais, d'un coeur aimant, etre la joie—I am to be a loving heart's chief joy. The ensemble opens tranquilly with Hero and Ursule, soon joined by Béatrice in expressing a shared bliss at Hero's impending wedding to her beloved Claudio. Hero and Ursule notice a mellowing in their friend, once so vehemently against marriage. To a quicker tempo, Béatrice insists still that marriage is not for her, growing increasingly agitated to the amusement of Ursule and alarm of Hero, who begins to worry aloud about Claudio and marriage generally. They calm down laughingly, then repeat the tranquil opening sequence in tight, sweet harmony. In addition to the beauty of the lyricism of the opening and closing sections, the composer's hair-trigger adherence to the moods of the three women is remarkable. Berlioz tracks their emotions, fast-moving and not easy to follow in the text, in what seems like real time.

Another serenade for an offstage chorus, accompanied by a guitar, serves as a gentle and charming summons to the wedding ceremony. As Hero and Ursule leave Béatrice alone onstage, Bénédict arrives, startling her. She resumes her insults. Speaking to himself, Bénédict admires her beauty and declares her abuse as proof of her love—these two are the picture of ambivalence. Claudio and Hero approach in a wedding march and chorus, Dieu qui guidas nos bras—God, who guided our arms—that has a different character than better-known examples by Mendelssohn and Wagner. Berlioz's approach is dignified and his tempo a bit slower. Two harps join the orchestra and, alongside the flutes and clarinets, gently dominate its sound. There's a gradual crescendo, which the composer then pulls back for a quiet closing. A bit of contrapuntal writing for the solo singers and chorus, Comble de tes faveurs ces deux nobles coeurs—Pour down thy favors on these two noble hearts—set over a pizzicato walking bass line for the cellos and double basses changes the texture and is of great beauty.

Don Pedro and Leonato congratulate Hero and Claudio but also unexpectedly—or not—reveal a second marriage contract, this of course for Béatrice and Bénédict. Once more the pair cannot stop their mutual teasing but finally agree to wed, as to a thunderous chorus comically echoing his curse on marriage in act 1 a shocked Bénédict declares: Ici l'on voit Bénédict, l'homme marié—Here you may see Bénédict the married man! Somarone unveils a sign bearing those words to be placed on his house.

Just two minutes long, the brilliant closing duet, L'amour est un flambeau—Love is a torch—carries the unusual title Scherzo duettino—jokelike little duet. The scampering, scurrying, leaping theme that dominates the overture returns, unmixed here with other material. The text is first sung in alternating lines, then together with Bénédict's description, to which Béatrice replies that it's une flame—a flame. They agree that love makes people crazy and that they'll go back to fighting tomorrow, which sentiment the other characters and chorus all cheer. The words seem tough-minded for the spinning fairy music they are set to; yet without question the finale is so brilliant—even dazzling—that it works, and it feels as though their marriage will too.

Goethean Drama
La Damnation de Faust

Berlioz began his composition of this masterpiece in 1845, finishing the following year. It's the direct descendant and heir of *Huit Scènes de* Faust—Eight Scenes from *Faust*—which he had composed in 1828 and 1829, published, then withdrew in dissatisfaction. Yet the earlier composition is absolutely excellent, and were it not expanded, enriched, and folded so skillfully into the later, greater conception, it would fully merit examination on its own as an early masterwork. It also represents a startling advance in invention and polish over the *Messe solennelle* of 1824. There's a great 2003 recording of the *Huit Scènes* with the Montreal Symphony Orchestra under Charles Dutoit. The eight carried over into *La Damnation de Faust* are referenced as they occur.

The legend of Faust, which goes back to the Middle Ages, was treated dramatically by Shakespeare's contemporary Christopher Marlowe in *The Tragical History of Doctor Faustus* (1604). Johann Wolfgang von Goethe (1749–1832), one of the giant figures of German and world literature, spent decades writing, rewriting, and expanding his *Faust*, a dramatic poem in two parts, publishing part 1 in 1806 and part 2 the year before his death. At the start of Goethe's part 1, Faust is a profound and brilliant old scholar of high accomplishment. But he's also disappointed with how he's spent his disciplined life, yearning for the sensual side he's steered clear of. Hearing his musings, Mephistopheles appears, offering to restore to Faust time, youth, and good looks in exchange for his soul. Faust makes the deal, then falls in love with Margarethe, nicknamed Gretchen, whose love for Faust and sexual awakening are portrayed with remarkable sympathy. Gretchen becomes involved with Faust in carnality and crime, for which she is imprisoned and condemned.

In the play's last moment, her salvation is announced by Heaven. The wide-ranging plot of part 2 is harder to summarize, but basically Faust is transported through time to witness remarkable figures and events. At the end Faust, once again old, is dying; Mephistopheles tries to make off with his soul, but Heaven claims it instead.

Although filled with ethical dilemmas and philosophical speculation, the clarity of Goethe's ideas and his aphoristic, pungent language come through well, even in translation. The influence of *Faust* on Western culture is incalculable: even those who know little about Goethe or his metaphysical drama understand that implicit in a "Faustian bargain" is the likelihood that the bettor will come to regret the deal.

The Faust legend's effect on music is enormous, with at least three operas on the subject, of which Gounod's saccharine *Faust* is probably the most familiar. In addition to writing several great songs to lyrics by Goethe, Schumann composed three unsatisfying fragments to unconnected scenes from parts 1 and 2. The second part of Mahler's Symphony No. 8 uses texts from *Faust*; Berlioz's friend Liszt also wrote his own take in *Eine Faust-Symphonie*—obviously, "A Faust Symphony." Of any and all, Berlioz's extraordinary dramatic cantata is the most compelling.

Since, in Goethe, both Faust and Gretchen are saved, the title *La Damnation* requires explanation, which the composer provides in a witty, unsigned, third-person introduction and apologia to the score. He explains that since the length and scope of the two dramatic poems precludes a complete musical setting, a selection of scenes had to be made. The composer chose, set, and organized what appealed to him; he then names some masterpieces by Mozart, Rossini, and Gluck, all of which come from literary sources that were altered and even mutilated to serve musical goals. As we'll see, Faust begins the process in part 2, when he agrees to Méphistophélès's proposal to change his life. He completes it formally in part 4, where in the hope of saving Marguerite, he signs in writing to serve his new master; and then, definitively, when he's delivered by Méphistophélès to hell.

The libretto is drawn mostly from the translation of *Faust* into French by Gérard de Nerval, published in 1827. Berlioz had an immediate and deep response: "I could not put it down, I read it incessantly, at meals, at the theatre, in the street."[34] But the final text is not purely Goethe in de Nerval's translation. To create new emphases, the composer interpolated some lines that without question add to his work's stature without detracting from Goethe at all: Faust's Invocation to Nature in part 4 is surely the finest example. Other instances serve more practical purposes, as in part 1, when Faust needs to explain his presence in Hungary, to prepare for the Marche Hongroise—Hungarian March—which may seem extraneous, but is made to fit the composer's overall conception.

There are almost fifty available recordings of *La Damnation*. The main characters are Faust, a juicy role for tenor that has been performed and recorded by some great voices, such as Stuart Burrows and Nicolai Gedda. Marguerite, the youthfully transformed Faust's lover and victim, is specified in the score as a mezzo-soprano but is also sung by sopranos. Here, too, singers of quality, including Janet Baker, Régine Crespin, and Marilyn Horne, have recorded this beautiful and moving role. At an opposite vocal pole from the lovers is Faust's tempter, Méphistophélès, who can be sung by a baritone or bass-baritone. This brilliant character role acts and sings in nearly constant opposition to the lovers' lyrical outpourings. Widely different voices have performed it successfully, from the light baritone Michel Roux to the more richly endowed bass-baritone Donald McIntyre. Brander, a tipsy student, sung by a bass, has a smaller but memorable scene in part 2. There's a big chorus, including children, and an orchestra with a slightly enlarged percussion section and four offstage brass instruments.

One of the questions that troubled the composer was how to categorize the work, which is neither opera nor symphony, though it contains elements of both. Ultimately, he settled on Légende dramatique en quatre parties—Dramatic legend in four parts—which works well. Divided into four sections of unequal length, the combined first and second run about ten minutes shorter than the third and fourth, making for a sensible division at halfway for live performances. Which, as for most of Berlioz's work, are shamefully rare. Each part is divided into scenes, mostly short, fast-moving, and varied in character. If ever the term *proto-cinematic* applied, it's here, as when Méphistophélès whisks Faust around; yet *Faust* seems ever modern, even timeless, in the way of a legend.

Another perpetual source of confusion is the fact that the score is full of stage directions, tempting directors to create semi- or full stagings of a work that stands on its own as a dramatic cantata. In fact, the composer toyed with the idea of expanding it into an opera, ultimately calling it "an opera without décor or costumes."[35] Perhaps the biggest flaw of *La Damnation de Faust* is its ending, where, after a bold, headlong work, and the particularly fine sequence that forms the first five scenes of part 4, heavenly choirs announce forgiveness for Marguerite's soul. It's a flat and disappointing conclusion to one of Berlioz's tightest masterpieces.

It may be hard to believe, but this great work was a failure at its two performances to half-empty halls in Paris in December 1846. Berlioz knew the value of his *Faust*, but was so discouraged that he considered stopping composing or leaving France for Germany or England, where he was more appreciated. In the decades following his death, and certainly by the early twentieth century, the stature of *La Damnation de Faust* had become clear.

Shortest of the four, part 1 acts as an introduction, albeit a strong one. In the opening number—there is no overture or prelude—Faust, on the "Plains of Hungary" for a reason that will soon be explained, soliloquizes gloriously. In a beautiful aria, Le vieil hiver—Old winter—the aged philosopher praises the spring and his solitude with an ardency that displays a still passionate character. The lilting theme with which Berlioz characterizes his protagonist and the changing season opens quietly in a single line for the violas joined contrapuntally by strings and winds, soon swelling into full-throated ecstasy. Busy but calm figuration for muted strings depict la brise matinale—morning breeze—welcomed by Faust, whose rocking melody retains its tranquility throughout. Distant woodwinds and muttered fanfares for the French horns introduce thematic ideas from the following two scenes. But Faust's glorious hymn returns, triumphant like a voice of nature, now for the orchestra alone.

The composer structures the Peasants' Dance (originally the second of the *Huit Scènes*) that follows as a beautifully gauged study in contrasts for the chorus and orchestra punctuated occasionally with comments by Faust. Opening with a scurrying choral narrative in 6/8 beat, Les bergers laissent leurs troupeaux—The shepherds leave their flocks—Berlioz then introduces the real country dance in 2/4 rhythm and a much quicker tempo, to tra-la las for the chorus, droning cellos that imitate bagpipes, and some wild decoration by the woodwinds. Murmuring dynamics tell us that they're at some distance. Faust, onstage, comments with envy on their untroubled lives; the low-volume country dance returns, enlivened by syncopations and more unexpected figuration for the woodwinds.

The third scene, which contains the Hungarian March—also known as the Rákóczy March—is probably the best-known passage in *Faust*. This wonderful orchestral showpiece is an interpolation by Berlioz. To explain why part 1 is set, unlike the original, in Hungary, Berlioz (as noted, writing in the third person) states, "The answer is simply because he wished to introduce a composition, the theme of which is Hungarian."[36] In a footnote he also comments that this movement is an elaboration on a Hungarian war-march of ancient origin, by an unknown composer.

The march itself, all swaggering affect, opens with loud fanfares from the heavy brass, but the catchy, charming main theme is set out quietly by the flutes and clarinets to a light, rhythmically flexible accompaniment that seems as much dance as march, with the choreographic feel keeping this section playful. Berlioz varies loud and soft passages in close contrast, also placing a milder-mannered major-key passage at the center. The percussion, including snare and bass drums and the triangle, is introduced gradually but maintains its showy presence to the cheerful bluster and rhythmic playfulness of the closing bars. Some conductors accelerate toward the end, but the composer gives no such instruction in the score.

The real drama begins with part 2, in the opening scene of which Faust, back in his gloomy study in gloomy northern Germany, laments his depression, then decides to end it all by drinking poison. In a noble, freely conceived monologue, Sans regrets j'ai quitté les riantes campagnes—Without regrets I left the smiling countryside—Berlioz depicts Faust's state of mind with a long, winding theme, starting in the cellos, which is then joined in free counterpoint by the lower strings and woodwinds. Bearing a family resemblance to material from *Harold en Italie*, the Requiem, and other works by the master, the twisting idea beautifully depicts the protagonist's melancholy, obsessive nature. At the end, it breaks into recitative as he prepares to die, at first resolutely, then in fear. Faust is interrupted by an Easter hymn, Christ vient de ressusciter—Christ has risen—which distracts, then saves him. (This was the first of the *Huit Scènes*.) Once again, the atheist Berlioz shows his gift at capturing a religious mood convincingly. The words are set to a fairly plain chorale tune that's exquisitely decorated, at first by the woodwinds in triplets, later by the violins and violas in quiet sixteenth notes. Faust's commentary is skillfully paced as he calms down and decides to live; three gorgeously exhaled Hosannas for the chorus end the scene.

In a short recitative, Faust wonders aloud why a welcome death was postponed; to a crunching three-note figure for bassoons, trumpets, and trombones, marked above by sharp whistling from the flutes and piccolo, Méphistophélès appears, commenting sarcastically, Ô pure émotion—Emotion of the soul—on the ease of Faust's reclamation to life and faith. In a brilliant, real-time dialogue in recitative punctuated by dry plucked strings and growling trombones, Méphistophélès identifies himself: Je suis l'esprit de vie—I am the spirit of life. He promises to fulfill all Faust's desires if he will just consent, which Faust does with little delay. Over scurrying strings the two are transported to Auerbach's cellar, a student tavern in Leipzig.

The remainder of part 2 consists of character pieces, all relatively short and of differing musical characters, as Méphistophélès whisks Faust to ostensibly pleasurable scenes and sights. The first four are deliberately rough, followed by three quieter, more sensitive settings, as Méphistophélès prepares his spiritual seduction of Faust.

The opening number, set in that Leipzig cellar, Oh! Qu'il fait bon—Oh, it's good—depicts not only the raucous atmosphere of the tavern but also, subtly, the hollow, alcohol-fueled good fellowship of the university students, with rackety brass fanfares and uneven choral lines. Brander, a drunken student, sings his witless and mildly off-color tale of a rat, Certain rat, dans une cuisine—There once was a rat in a kitchen (fourth of the *Huit Scènes*). The gist of the story is that the rat is in such torment after eating poison that she acts as if she's in heat; when she runs desperately into the oven, she's really cooked. Although Berlioz's treatment is less noisy than that for the opening chorus, it's still rough, in keeping with the text, with the orchestral accompaniment dominated by gurgling bassoons and quick figuration for the strings between verses. Rough as well, although in fact a sophisticated musical joke, is the ironic Amen chorus by the students for the dead rat that follows. Berlioz loathed showy choral Amens at the end of otherwise admirable musical settings of the Mass. Here he parodies them without mercy in a loud, heavy, fugue for the men's chorus.

The students are not too drunk to notice the mockery in Méphistophélès's praise of their counterpoint. Nevertheless, they allow him to sing the next song, Une puce gentille—A lovely flea—more commonly referred to as the Song of the Flea (fifth of the *Huit Scènes*), which is nasty in a different way. This fable tells of a flea who makes friends with a prince, who then welcomes the flea's relatives; since it's hard to complain about parasites with powerful friends, it's best to crush them quickly. The composer's skill at satirical tone painting is on full display, with strings depicting the leaping, biting insects and the scratching courtiers, as well as four-note explosions that add the brass and timpani at the ends of each verse depicting the swatting and crushing of the insects, both literal and figurative. This number is also remarkable for its compression and concision, with all three verses dispatched in about ninety seconds.

Of course, none of this is what Faust desired in the way of new experience, and he tells his Guide infernal—Satanic guide—to take him to a calmer place. This Méphistophélès accomplishes to some of the score's most proto-cinematic music, filled with metrically shifting scales for the strings and buzzing trills for the woodwinds. Berlioz has led the characters to a moment of repose at the banks of the River Elbe. Here he sings Faust a lullaby, Voici les roses—Here are roses—fogging his victim's senses with sleep and, later, desire for Marguerite. Although unmistakably a lullaby, and a gorgeous one, Berlioz scores it with surprising weight, cornets and trombones dominating the sound. Méphistophélès then summons spirits to lull Faust to sleep and coax him to dream of Marguerite as he lays his trap.

That the fairy music of Faust's dream (originally number three of the *Huit Scènes*) is of extraordinary delicacy and beauty will be obvious to first-time listeners, but further acquaintance deepens respect.

Moving at a moderate tempo, and rarely loud, the chorus murmurs dors—sleep—as Méphistophélès sings gently that Une beauté . . . t'aimera—A beautiful girl . . . will love you. The hypnosis works, as Faust sings Marguerite's name in passionate tones. Berlioz's orchestral mastery is on full display with two of his favorite instruments, the English horn and viola, presenting the initial long-spun melodic idea. The composer thickens his textures a bit but keeps them airy and open as the passage progresses. Silvery scales for muted violins and violas lead to the end, which is linked to the dance that follows; Méphistophélès praises his minions for their work. The mood evoked by Faust's dream is too magical to shatter, so the Dance of the Sylphs serves as its exquisite orchestral pendant. Scored for woodwinds, strings, and harp, its long, mincing melody has an almost toylike quality. A single note—D—is held from the first bar to the last by the cellos and double basses, but the stability that the long-held D might provide is undermined by rhythmic shifts and unexpected sinking chromatic drops in the melody and its harmonic background. It would be surprising if this fine-boned waltz were not very familiar to Tchaikovsky.

To an orchestral eruption Faust wakes, calling for Marguerite, the woman of his dreams. Méphistophélès promises that Faust will hold her in his arms today, then suggests they join a passing crowd of soldiers and students that will approach her house. This concerted number, which features both soldiers and students singing in competing polyphony, opens at low volume with pizzicato strings and a falling figure for the bassoons. The soldiers, entering first, sing sturdily of their duty to defend the town, which, as they see, will be rewarded by Fillettes sucrées aux malins regards, victoire certaine près de vous m'attend—Sweet girls, to the mischievous eyes [that show] certain victory awaits me by your side. This soldiers' march has unusual energy, supplied by Berlioz's bouncing rhythm; fanfares for trumpets and cornets give a more predictable military feel to the accompaniment. The students enter, singing of the same goal, but in double-entendre Latin and a different meter. More difficult to set, the Latin sounds breathless and garbled, making the march more appealing musically; soon both are singing at the same time in a rhythmic competition that's too obvious. Following a loud climax for soldiers, students, and orchestra, there's a long diminuendo for strings and bassoons that parallels the opening sequence. Although one of Berlioz's trademark techniques, this fade-down comes as a welcome surprise after the boisterous passage it follows. And the whole concluding ensemble, while not always pleasant listening, serves an important purpose, as it foreshadows Faust's conquest of Marguerite.

Berlioz continues his story with military music, opening part 3 with call-and-response fanfares for cornets, French horns, and timpani, some onstage, others off, in a carefully gauged diminuendo. Now inside Marguerite's room, Faust sings a tender aria, Merci, doux crepuscule—Thanks, gentle twilight—to his idealized lover and the joy she's already giving him, even though they've yet to meet. (Also ironic is Faust's relief that his suffering has finally ended, though he will soon abandon her.) But certainly, Berlioz's melody, set over muted strings that suggest the soft light of dusk, with gentle lines for the flutes, clarinets, and English horn, is irresistibly warm, moving freely with the nuances of the text. The composer adds a long postlude in steady eighth notes to depict Faust's wonder and bliss as he wanders slowly through Marguerite's room, as the stage directions in the score indicate. The singer's part is difficult, notable for a high note (A-flat) to be sung very softly following a short pause. High notes are more easily approached without breaks in the vocal line, and require much greater control when sung pianissimo than in full voice.

A densely packed recitative, in which samples of themes yet unheard are presented, sets the next scene. Introduced again with his barking trombone motif, Méphistophélès alerts Faust of Marguerite's approach. A clarinet introduces fragments of the melody of her aria, Le Roi de Thulé—The king of Thule which follows; a lively tune for pizzicato strings then samples Méphistophélès's serenade, also to follow. Following the composer's stage direction, Marguerite enters, Faust hides, and Méphistophélès exits. Lyrical lines for flutes and clarinets are underpinned by a more active figure for violas below, which tells of her agitation. Her first line, Que l'air est étouffant—How stuffy the air is—makes for a remarkable entrance both musically and dramatically. She recalls, to a surging melody, last night's dream of a handsome lover before dismissing it as nonsense.

Berlioz gives her aria (Le Roi de Thulé, sixth of the *Huit Scènes* and Track 4) the subtitle *Chanson gothique*, which one score translates as "Medieval Song."[37] The Middle Ages were scorned as an era of ignorance and superstition during the Enlightenment, and the more or less parallel classical period in the arts, but by the nineteenth century, European cultures took a renewed interest in and liking to the period. There are many examples of romanticized medievalism, of which Wagner's *Lohengrin* will be familiar to many; Marguerite's haunting aria is another. There's nothing genuinely medieval about Berlioz's method or sound. Rather, he achieves an archaic feeling chiefly by means of the folklike cast of the melody, its harmonic background, and the subject itself, which has the ring of antiquity. Its six verses tell a sad and straightforward tale of marital loyalty: an old king never lets go of a golden cup given him by his late, well-loved wife. At a banquet, he throws it into the sea, then lies down, ready to die.

Berlioz's treatment, astonishing for its somber containment, is created by its dark scoring, soft dynamics, and, as noted, the folklike melody and harmony. The composer gives his beloved viola dominance in the strings, using one soloist accompanied by a singular ensemble of six violas, with cellos and double basses below, and notably, no violins. The winds, consisting of flutes, clarinets, and four French horns, play quiet but crucial roles. The aria opens almost inaudibly with plucked double basses, then the winds, which set the harmony. The solo viola presents the first line of the melody, presented by the clarinet in fragments in the introductory recitative. Marguerite sings the opening verse, Autrefois une roi de Thulé, qui jusqu'au tombeau fut fidèle—There was a king of Thule who was faithful unto death—following the violist. So tight in range and austere is the melody that all deviations make a powerful effect, as when the vocal line dips just a bit to describe the king's emotion when, a sa vue humectait ses yeux—at the mere sight of the cup, a tear moistened his eye. The solo viola is the singer's companion throughout, foreshadowing and echoing her line, with the other six violas holding to a rocking accompaniment. Also worth listening for is the mournful, two-note falling figure for the flutes. Once the king's death has been narrated, Marguerite, to whose restless lover this tale will stand in bitter contrast, repeats the opening line to a disintegrating accompaniment, then sighs deeply.

Speaking of the Middle Ages, the interval Berlioz employs (the fourth) as Méphistophélès summons his minions, Esprits des flames inconstantes, accourez—Spirits of fickle flame, come quickly—is so unstable to Western ears that it has been described as the *diabolus in musica*—the devil in music—since that era. Composers use it regularly to suggest sinister activity or, as in Bernstein's *West Side Story*, to create a powerful musical or dramatic tension. Called to complete his plot against Faust and Marguerite, the spirits' arrival is depicted by scurrying winds and strings, marked by occasional explosive accents as Méphistophélès threatens them if they fail in their mission.

The Menuet des Follets—Dance of the Will o' the Wisps—that follows is a substantial ballet movement that's superficially charming, but in fact quite unsettling. Berlioz bases the dance on four thematic ideas, which he breaks, often abruptly, and blends freely. The static opening theme, assigned to the woodwinds and brass, suggests less than its development, particularly by means of the orchestration, will show; but even here, harmonic shifts and rhythmic hiccups subvert any sense of choreographic fluidity. The second theme, given to the strings, sharply punctuated by the woodwinds, is underlined by a moan for the French horns. The first and second themes are blended, but also interrupted by huge climaxes and long pauses for the full orchestra and the gradual addition of the percussion. The third thematic idea, a long-limbed melody for the violins, is distracted by nervous skittering in the high woodwinds, leading to more huge and startling chords for the full orchestra, and ultimately, the fourth theme, which seems to come from nowhere. In the character of a fast country dance, at a much quicker tempo, this theme is notable for its sharply marked short-short-long rhythm, taken by piccolos and flutes, accompanied by plucked strings. There's some playful commentary by the bassoons, and more ominous tones from the trombones. Berlioz recapitulates most of the themes briefly and brilliantly, but again with a violent undertone, then ends unexpectedly with a graceful trill for the violins.

In the short recitative that follows, Berlioz instructs Méphistophélès to "imitate a hurdy-gurdy player," meaning to turn his forearm and hand in a circular motion. The mechanical, stringed hurdy-gurdy dates back to the Middle Ages; once a familiar instrument for street performers, its droning timbre has been exploited by composers from Schubert (Der Leiermann—The Hurdy-Gurdy Man—the last number of the despairing song cycle *Winterreise*, "Winter's Journey") to Donovan, the folk-rock singer and writer of another gloomy song (from 1968) with the same title. In fact, the effect imitates a guitar, which instrument serves as the singer's sole accompaniment in the song's first version in *Huit Scènes*, rather than a hurdy-gurdy. (It's uncertain why the composer mentions the hurdy-gurdy in the score, as the guitar is the instrument actually used in the *Huit Scènes*, and imitated by the orchestra in *Faust*.)

Hoping to clinch Marguerite's fall, Méphistophélès, accompanied by a male chorus of spirits, sings his serenade, Devant la maison de celui qui t'adore—Before the house of him who adores you—a concerted number that is a stunning display of sonority, compression and momentum (and eighth of the *Huit Scènes*). The archlike melody is backed by that undulating, guitarlike string accompaniment that's a miracle on its own, with some plucking while others play arpeggiated (broken) chords. It's also marked with two sharp laughs for Méphistophélès and chorus, both set to one sharply accented note, accompanied by the only big chord in the serenade. Berlioz ends the verses and precedes the laughs with a condensed version of the strings' undulations, for comically gurgling woodwinds, which also add falling figures in detached notes, contributing another, more playful instrumental laugh. The text takes more than one posture about premarital sex, warning its generic object, Petite Luison—Little Louisa: Au signal du plaisir, dans la chambre du drille tu peux bien entrer fille, mais non fille en sortir—When pleasure calls, into his room you may enter a virgin, but you'll not come out one. Yet, a couple of swift verses later, she's advised to get un anneau conjugal—a wedding ring—first.

Berlioz prefaces the love duet for Faust and Marguerite with a recollection of the tune of Le Roi de Thulé, here by the oboes. Marguerite is, naturally, startled to find Faust in her room; but he begins his declaration, Ange adoré—Beloved angel—in full-throated passion, to a tender melody accompanied by muted strings. Marguerite expresses surprise that he knows her name, although she admits shyly to knowing his. The lovers sing passionately almost from the start, their vocal lines sometimes alternating closely, others sweetly harmonized, with her often taking the lower note. Marguerite, already in love, won't hide her passion, addressing him almost immediately as mon bien aimé—my beloved. The instrumental accompaniment becomes more elaborate, as flutes and clarinets decorate the melodic lines in detached notes. Berlioz captures the text with a triumphant phrase as the pair reach agreement that love has swept aside all doubt or hesitation: Ton amour est vainqueur—Your love has driven [them] away. Moments later, as the new experience of physical desire overtakes Marguerite, the composer tracks her words Quelle langueur s'empare de mon être—What languor seizes my being—characterizing these primal feelings with rumbling from the cellos and double basses far below.

Accompanied by big chords for the full orchestra, Méphistophélès interrupts, warning of the approach of a crowd that has heard them and is calling for Marguerite's mother to hurry home and save her daughter's virtue. Marguerite instinctively dreads Méphistophélès. Faust is not easily persuaded to leave now, continuing to express his passion, Adieu, donc, belle nuit—Farewell then, sweet night—even after Marguerite tells him to go. Amid orchestral bustle and interruptions by Méphistophélès, they furtively make plans to meet again tomorrow. The crowd is finally heard in the distance, leading to a quick-tempo ensemble for the principals and chorus in which Marguerite manages to sing lyrically of her love of Faust, who looks ahead to bliss with this beautiful woman: Je connais donc enfin tout le prix de la vie—At last I know life's prize—while Méphistophélès crows that Faust's soul will soon be his. Later, the approaching crowd joins in, leading to an accelerated, wild ending reminiscent of the final moments of the *Symphonie fantastique*. The crowd scene, with some form of danger on the way, is a convention borrowed straight from opera. While one of the less lovable parts of Berlioz's conception, it's well put together and concise, like so much of *Faust*.

Part 4 opens with a lament by Marguerite, whom Faust has left behind in his search for new experience, and seventh of the *Huit Scènes*. Grandly proportioned and beautifully executed, Berlioz reveals Marguerite's warmth and a nobility in her suffering. The aria D'amour l'ardente flame—The burning flame of love—makes for an interesting comparison with Schubert's setting of the same text. That song, "Gretchen am Spinnrade" ("Gretchen at the Spinning Wheel") is one of that composer's greatest, capturing her erotic despair with rare acuity by means of the piano accompaniment—which imitates the movement of the wheel, depicting her obsession musically—and his placement of the musical and dramatic climax on her memory of Faust's kiss. Berlioz takes a different approach, but his interpretation of Goethe's text is no less fine.

Set in sections of alternating character, thematic ideas are often varied, but one, the unforgettable melody of Marguerite's initial statement returns mostly unaltered. Her instrumental partner throughout is the sad English horn, which presents her great melody four times in full, also adding mournful but thematically relevant commentary with phrases adapted from the melody along the way. The aria opens with the rueful melody, presented by the English horn with soft harmonic backing from the strings, broken by five brief pauses and marked by a painfully wide leap. When the singer starts, the cellos and double basses join with gentle pulsations. With the words Alors ma pauvre tête se dérange bientôt—So my poor head soon loses its senses—the strings join in a steadier pulsation; as she recalls his good looks and noble bearing, the accompaniment shifts to syncopations for the strings and a more fluid vocal line. Berlioz, like Schubert, emphasizes her memory of his kiss, changing the meter in the middle of her recollection, Hélas! Et son baiser!—And, alas, his kiss! Again, the setting changes pace as she imagines hearing him at her window or door, this to a vocal line that's fragmented to depict her agitation, echoed by the fluttering, broken phrases in the strings. Now possessed by passionate memory (O caresses de flame—Oh, caresses of fire) Marguerite breaks into a slow recitative, accompanied by trembling strings, woodwinds exhaling gently, and some carnal grunts from the double basses. To a falling figure for muted violins, the English horn reiterates the melody, more painfully expressive than ever after Marguerite's confession.

The spaciousness of Berlioz's conception can be seen in his way of closing the aria. Demonstrating that life outside Marguerite's and Faust's love has continued, drums and trumpets repeat the fanfares from the opening of part 3; soldiers and students repeat phrases from their competing choruses, as Marguerite painfully recalls the night Où l'amour offrit à mes yeux—When love brought [Faust] to me—then repeats, twice, as she has had to for some time now, Il ne vient pas—He's not coming. As the English horn plays its lament one last time, she sings Hélas—Alas—twice in nearly mute despair.

The last examples of noble behavior by Faust were in part 1; ever since he's acted like a spoiled adolescent. But the next number, his Invocation to Nature (Track 5), restores some sense of what made him interesting. The text, which opens with: Nature immense, impénétrable et fière—Nature, vast, unfathomable, proud—is not by Goethe and is, as noted, the work of the composer himself.[38] An impressive specimen of romantic nature worship on its own, this rhyming poem also captures Faust's fatal flaw, the ennui sans fin—unending ennui—that prevents him from appreciating anything for long, including Marguerite.

In another scene shift that foreshadows cinema, we're transported to "woods and cavern" where Faust apostrophizes the only thing that impresses him, or seems to, for now. Broad, majestic, and free, the musical setting matches the text marvelously; with rich, dark-hued orchestration and ever-shifting harmony, the passage echoes the music of Faust's opening aria in ways both clear and subtle. Berlioz leaves regular melody aside for this grand recitative, accompanied by the full orchestra and set, like so many of his best ideas, in 9/8 meter. The music speaks well enough for itself, but listen for the surging line for bassoons, cellos, and double bass that punctuates the music like the wind invoked by Faust: Oui, soufflez, ouragans—Yes, blow, hurricanes—painting majestically in tone irregular and uncontrollable natural forces. There's a hint of a melodic turn as Faust tries to meld his voice into the surrounding turmoil, and a climax for Faust's vocal line on his final words, D'un coeur trop vaste et d'une âme altérée d'un bonheur qui la fuit—Of a heart too vast, a longing soul, of a fleeting happiness[39]—where he admits despairingly that not even Nature fills his emptiness. The composer winds this admirable passage down quietly, moodily, and without fuss.

Méphistophélès joins Faust, provoking him with a sarcastic question about faithful love. This opens an important transitional dialogue in recitative, in which the two male leads are characterized vividly. Throughout the scene, hunting horns are heard in the distance, as Méphistophélès notes early on. Symbolizing his hunt for Faust's soul, they are heard as the background of this entire short but intense sequence. On paper, the concept may sound contrived, but it works.

When Méphistophélès mentions Marguerite, Faust guiltily yells at him to shut up. Méphistophélès then relates that she has been condemned for the murder of her mother, who died from the sleeping potion Marguerite gave her to facilitate her trysts with Faust: Marguerite is now to die for her love of Faust. Faust tries to blame his tempter, who will have none of it. Méphistophélès can free Marguerite, but Faust must sign to serve him from then on, marked by the horns with a single soft chord, but muted and in the minor key. Faust signs, immediately and impulsively, to one soft, ominous strike of the tamtam, a large gong. Faust says they must hurry to the prison, opening a thrilling musical sequence.

Proto-cinematic indeed is the Journey to the Abyss, the extraordinary passage depicting the wild ride of Faust and Méphistophélès across increasingly fantastical and terrifying earthly landscapes, and "operatic" also applies. (It's Track 6.) The composer depicts with some of his most vivid tone painting the galloping of the black horses summoned by Méphistophélès, ostensibly to rush them to save Marguerite, but actually to drop Faust, his new possession, in hell. The movement of the hell-bound horses is depicted in a relentless (long-short-short) rhythm but with all the notes moving quickly. A solo oboe floats above in a long-limbed, asymmetrical, expressive lament, functioning separately from the galloping strings but working brilliantly alongside them. Throughout, the cellos and double basses track one thematic idea or another, but never synchronize fully with any.

Faust expresses his pain for Marguerite's situation. The riders approach some peasants kneeling at a wayside cross, whom Faust symbolically would not disturb; Méphistophélès insists that they must keep their pace, causing the spectral women and children to scatter in fear. Berlioz begins to introduce low-pitched instruments, starting with bassoons and trombones but off the beat and in notes far from the main tonality, tightening the nightmarish dread. Faust imagines night birds, depicted by chattering high woodwinds, chasing them, and begins, late in the game (like Mozart's Don Giovanni), to express his fear. There's a momentary pause as Méphistophélès asks Faust whether he wants to turn back, telling his soon-to-be victim that he hears the bell tolling Marguerite's execution. Faust presses on, resuming the wild ride, with Méphistophélès driving the horses continually as Faust hallucinates skeletons grinning and nodding as they pass and a rain of blood. Now at the brink of hell, Méphistophélès summons his minions d'une voix tonnante—with a thundering voice—as he and Faust, who cries in open terror, tumble together into the abyss of hell.

The original meaning of Pandaemonium—the title of this scene—in its specific, Miltonic sense in book 1 of *Paradise Lost* is the abode of demons, or the capital of hell; later usage has come to describe any wild or chaotic scene. Berlioz's musical depiction of hell is a first cousin of the Dies irae in the Requiem, with brass thundering in convulsive rhythms. Faust is now an anonymous citizen of hell; only Méphistophélès and his troop remain. The demons, in chorus, sing in a made-up demonic tongue (one sample: Irimiru karabrako) to welcome their chief. They ask ritualistically whether Faust signed of his own free will, to which Méphistophélès answers, Il signa librement—He signed freely. He's then carried triumphantly on their shoulders to a wild, quick march as they sing, which then shifts to a crazed but charming dance. One last hectic passage ends with five big chords in a sinking harmonic pattern as a solo bass (in some performances a small group of basses) narrates the opening of the Epilogue, in which Faust's absorption into hell is described. The scene in Pandaemonium has been great fun to hear, as, pulling away cinematically from the demons and their wild behavior, the narrator somberly points out, Dans ses profoundeurs un mystère d'horreur s'accomplit—In its depths a frightful mystery was performed.

Strings and harps are already in celestial mode as a chorus of high voices asks God to forgive Marguerite. One soprano calls her name, leading to her Apotheosis, in which Berlioz continues his high-pitched, delicate orchestration, initially for drastically reduced strings, which he increases imperceptibly as the music moves forward, also joined toward the end by a children's chorus. The heavenly chorus sings that she's forgiven because Que l'amour l'égara—She was led astray by love. Toward the end, the chorus invites her to come as the soprano calls her name, ending this remarkable score quietly if unconvincingly. The quality and vigor even of what precedes it in part 4 puts the Apotheosis, well executed though it may be, at a disadvantage. Also, it seems like scant comfort to modern, secular audiences that Marguerite has been executed and only her soul forgiven.

As with Verdi, death scenes in which characters sing of the approach of heaven often have a perfunctory quality, perhaps not surprising considering that he, like Berlioz, was an atheist. But dramatic music of that era offers countless examples of sugar-coated death scenes. As one commentator notes, "Here in particular we must try to listen with nineteenth-century ears and be thankful that the music is not as saccharine as it might have been in other hands."[40]

Sacred Music, Part 1
The Rediscovered *Messe solennelle*, the *Te Deum*, and *L'Enfance du Christ*

As we know, Berlioz was not religious. His *Memoirs* are clear about his attitude, as background and in countless specifics. Although his relationship with each parent was troubled, he had more sympathy with his physician father, a man of science and a doubter, than his mother, who was pious but mean-spirited.[41] His dislike for the Catholic Church is summarized in this much-repeated, wittily distilled, comment on the first page of the *Memoirs*: "This charming religion (so attractive since it gave up burning people) was for seven whole years the joy of my life, and although we have since fallen out, I have always kept the most tender memories of it."[42]

It's fair to ask why a doubter like Berlioz wrote such great religious music. The answer may be simply that religion was still a potent source of musical and dramatic inspiration for him; moreover, it was material he had been hearing repeatedly and thinking about since childhood. Perhaps he was ready to write the Requiem because the qualities inherent in how man faces death appealed to the humanist in him, and to the dramatist, too.

Messe solennelle (Solemn Mass)

Berlioz claimed to have burned this piece, except for one section, the Resurrexit, which he rewrote. But in a rare and thrilling case of the rediscovery of an important work by a major composer, the complete score, in the composer's own hand, was found in 1991 in the organ loft of a church in Antwerp, Belgium, by Frans Moors, an organist and choirmaster. The cover contained an inscription by Antoine Bessems, a Conservatoire classmate, violinist, and longtime friend of Berlioz's. Moors contacted Hugh Macdonald, a British musicologist and Berlioz expert, who verified the score as the composer's long-missing Mass, his earliest large-scale work. The first performance of its second life was given in 1993, led by John Eliot Gardiner.

The twenty-year-old Berlioz composed the Mass in 1824. The work was performed twice in Paris, in 1825 and 1827. Like most early Berlioz, its daring qualities were obvious and the work was well received. But soon the composer himself found it weak, having progressed considerably in his own training, skill, and broadened musical experience. Saving and recasting what he considered the best part (the Resurrexit), he disavowed the Mass, and claimed to have destroyed it, along with other early efforts. When he started his *Memoirs* twenty-five years or more afterward, he probably forgot the copy of the work he'd given to Bessems.

Berlioz himself may have outgrown his *Messe solenelle*, but its rediscovery has given the world a seminal work. Remarkable, too, for a late starter whose serious training had barely begun. It's quite predictive of the composer's development and ambitious for a natural musician whose formal training was minimal, showing his flair for dramatic gesture, with some natural feel for pacing and contrast over a long musical span. While the *Messe* has with plenty of flaws, it's enjoyable for its raw, youthful energy, and as a display of the composer's unfettered imagination. The seven borrowings Berlioz made for later works are startling to hear in this context, demonstrating that some of his most inspired thematic ideas came early. As we'll see, excellent material was recycled in the Requiem, *Benvenuto Cellini*, the *Carnaval romain* overture, the Te Deum, and the *Symphonie fantastique*.

Most musical settings of the Mass by Bach, Haydn, Mozart, and Beethoven follow a familiar pattern of six large movements: Kyrie, Gloria, Credo, Sanctus, Benedictus, and Agnus Dei, with shorter subsections. Composers give prominence to the parts that appeal to them. Young Berlioz breaks his out differently, adding three sections. Those who have heard one or two musical settings of the Mass will spot the orchestral introduction, the Motet O salutaris, and closing Domine, salvum as the additions. As one might expect, the last, a prayer for the King of France, was common in Masses of the era by French composers; the introduction and motet are additions of the composer's own.

The orchestral introduction is short but enjoyable for its sequences of falling strings in syncopation. The actual opening liturgy—the sacred text of the Mass, its libretto or script—the Kyrie—is set in three parts, with Berlioz following tradition in tone and proportion. The fearful entreaty to God the stern father contrasts with that to Christ, in a more tender and hopeful tone. The opening entreaty Kyrie eleison—Lord, have mercy—is set to a somber theme Berlioz would redeploy in a slightly altered but completely recognizable form as the primary idea of the Offertorium in the Requiem. His manner of working it through there is, of course, more sophisticated, but here it's still pretty ear-catching. As in the Requiem, the composer's treatment of this plea is polyphonic. The central section, Christe eleison—Christ, have mercy—has a melting sweetness, with a switch to a major key and soaring lines for the strings and chorus. With accelerating tempos and pounding timpani, all in a long crescendo, the return of the Kyrie leads to a wild climax. A startling shift to the major key introduces Berlioz the musical dramatist.

More characteristic ideas appear throughout the next part, the Gloria in excelsis Deo—Glory to God on high—with the widely spaced woodwind chords that open it being one. Strings bustle excitedly to prepare for the joyful cries of the chorus on the opening line. Over murmuring for the male chorus, the women sing Laudamus te, benedicamus te, glorificamus te—We praise Thee, bless Thee, worship Thee—to another of the composer's great tunes to be recycled, the irregular and beautiful melody best known as the climactic idea of the overture *Le Carnaval romain*, and much less so for its presence in act 1 of *Benvenuto Cellini*. After the initial surprise, one finds it works well here, too. Some hiccups for the female singers reflect the composer's inexperience but also have an undeniable charm. In another stylistic trademark, Berlioz builds in an accelerating passage for the full ensemble, then ends gracefully on quiet chords: Adoramus te—We adore Thee.

Another big hit of the future forms the basis of the next section, Gratias agimus tibi—We give thanks to thee. Listeners familiar with the *Symphonie fantastique* but not this work will be surprised to hear the main theme of the third movement spun out in pristine glory. The young Berlioz already displays his characteristic technique of floating the long melody in the violins and clarinets without accompaniment or harmonization, letting his remarkable inspiration take its time, fully one minute of a passage that only runs under seven. There's another minute of harmonized melody before the chorus joins, and a ninety-second orchestral postlude. The references to timings are to show that this beautiful movement is as concise as its descendant of 1830 is long. Of course, by then Berlioz puts it to different and more ambitious use, but this exquisite passage seems closer to perfection.

Berlioz came to despise the choral fugue on Quoniam tu solus sanctus—For Thou alone are holy—commenting, "This execrable fugue must be rewritten"[43] on its first page in this manuscript. The "execrable fugue" is a short, brisk interpretation that doesn't sound that bad. More obviously awkward is the Credo in unum Deum—I believe in one God—a wordy, abstract text that needed a more experienced hand than the young composer's. Set for the bass soloist and chorus, certain phrases demonstrate Berlioz's sensitivity to words and his gift for setting declamatory text.

The setting of Et incarnatus est—And was made incarnate—has a naive charm that anticipates *L'Enfance du Christ*. Set for soprano and bass soloist, the French horns, cellos, and flutes burble along blissfully as accompaniment. The Crucifixus etiam pro nobis—And was crucified for us—is taut and dramatic, opening with stabbing accents and screeching, dissonant chords for the woodwinds interspersed with tense silences. The rest of the tragic text is given to the chorus over a chromatically sinking bass line that's more conventional but well handled. The closing bars start quietly, then shift to drama with shocking chords and a soft, rising figure in a major key that vividly depicts the moment of Christ's resurrection.

Central to Berlioz's vision and most fertile for themes that reappeared later in his career is the Resurrexit tertia die—On the third day He rose again. The chorus enters excitedly over a galloping figure. Within seconds, to Et ascendit in coelum—And ascended to heaven—

they move into longer notes suspended over dense pizzicato strings, a moment of stunning beauty, remarkable for its maturity. As we'll see, the composer recycled it twenty-five years later in the Christe, Rex Gloria movement of the Te Deum. Brass fanfares signal a slowdown that directly anticipates the Tuba mirum of the Requiem of 1837. Although much elaborated in the later work, the ancestry is clear. The composer speeds up for a contrapuntal setting of Et iterum venturus—And he shall come again—to a memorable, winding melody that reappears in the finale to act 1 of *Benvenuto Cellini*. Berlioz works it into an impressive quasi-operatic ensemble that's misplaced in this sacred work. Moving toward the Requiem, the composer saved and revised this movement, adding a phrase of text from that liturgy.

Motet is an old-fashioned, generic term for a vocal composition with a nonliturgical text.[44] Taking a passage from Exodus, Quis similis tui . . . Domine?—Who is like unto thee . . . Lord?—Berlioz's is one of his own interpolations into the Mass. Set for bass and chorus in an old-fashioned dotted (short-*long*) rhythm, it reminds some of Handel in its brisk pace and stately bearing. Brisk, busy, and compact might also describe the Sanctus—Holy—that follows. The prayer to Christ, O salutaris—O savior—isn't found in every musical setting of the Mass. Toward its end, the composer introduces two harps into its open textures. How well they fit is questionable, but their light touch seems inoffensive.

Agnus Dei, qui tollis peccata mundi—Lamb of God, who takes away the sins of the world—is cast, like settings by other masters, in a tone of remorseful entreaty. Sung by the tenor soloist, it's set to a throbbing, carefully phrased (short-short-long) accompaniment that runs from the first bar to the end. The soprano chorus joins the soloist in murmuring, even notes toward the end, where Berlioz shifts in its last moments from the minor tonality to the relative major, offering a bit of hope from the prevailing mood of repentance. This movement was also transferred, nearly intact, to the Te Deum. The final section, Domine, salvum fac regem nostrum—Lord, save our king—opens and ends with a setting that's rousing and even raw, but a quieter passage at its center with melting suspensions for the chorus over pizzicatos in the low strings provides contrast.

Te Deum

An ancient hymn to God and Christ, the Te Deum has been set to music many times over the centuries. Popular and adaptable to different interpretations, it was treated compactly though beautifully by many Renaissance composers, including the gloomy Spaniard Tomás Luis de Victoria and the English masters Thomas Tallis, William Byrd, and Orlando Gibbons. During the baroque era, the Te Deum came to be used to celebrate moments of national victory in more extended and ceremonial settings. Handel composed three, the last called the Dettingen Te Deum, to honor a defeat of the French army by England in 1743. There are also important settings by Haydn and Verdi.

Berlioz wrote this big occasional work in 1848 with no specific event in mind. Nineteenth-century France was often at war, and a victory might always be on the horizon. He himself led its first performance on April 28, 1855, in a large church in Paris for the opening of a world's fair–like festival. It's therefore in a spirit of national thanksgiving that Berlioz's Te Deum, widely recognized as a descendant of the Requiem, is cast. The composer adds a huge choral group, including a separate chorus of children and an organ, although the orchestra is the normal size. (As we'll see in chapter 7, the Requiem has instrumental groups that are considerably expanded.) According to the composer's instructions, the children's chorus is to be "as numerous as possible."[45] He deploys this element in three of the six choral movements, to greatest effect in the last. As in the Requiem, Berlioz moves the text around freely to suit structural purposes. While the Te Deum is less overtly dramatic than the Requiem, the composer is still intent on exploiting contrasting moods suggested by the words, with everything building toward the conflict-laden closing section, the Judex crederis—We believe You will come to be our judge.

Like the more familiar Requiem, the Te Deum is a big-boned piece that's rarely performed. The sense of vastness it unquestionably imparts may be the result of its big choruses, unhurried pacing, and musical density, because it's not all that long, running under an hour in either of its two versions. Berlioz composed two sections to be used only at a service of thanksgiving, in celebration of a big national victory. These extra movements show just how specific the composer's plans for the work were, with two recordings making the point. The first, a 1982 performance led by Claudio Abbado, runs forty-six minutes; the second, from 2001, conducted by John Nelson, clocks in at fifty-seven. Nelson includes the two "optional" sections; Abbado doesn't, accounting for the difference. Of course, we'll look at both movements.

The Te Deum may be big-boned, but it's also exceedingly fine-grained. To follow the composer's output chronologically is to hear in this work something new and more austere, with the wildness of the Requiem, the *Symphonie fantastique*, and *Harold en Italie* vanished, along with most of the miscalculations and outright blunders. Instead there's a new technical mastery and far higher degree of polish. The Te Deum may not be likable in the way of those earlier works, since it's less personal, and not intended for likability, per se:

> Berlioz's late style, which begins with the Te Deum, is best defined as a new embrace of classical, ultimately conservative ideals, reflected not just in the subject matter but also in the composer's disciplined restraint of musical materials and pronounced terseness of design . . . A new *hauteur* [haughtiness, which in French also entails nobility of manner or bearing] is to be seen in the music, a loftiness, a detachment.[46]

Yet, like so much of this composer's work, familiarity will be rewarded with respect and admiration that grow with each listening.

The work opens with a proclamatory sequence of alternating chords for the orchestra and the organ, setting at once the work's huge scale. The organ lays out part of the sturdy, choralelike fugue subject that the chorus sets forth: Te Deum laudamus, te Dominum confitemur—We praise thee, God; we acknowledge you as Lord. Closely overlapping entries early in the passage are of ear-catching radiance. The score moves into darker tonal territory with longer-held notes and shadowed harmonies for Omnis terra veneratur—All the earth worships you—set in hesitant phrases. The choral fugue resumes with busier orchestral accompaniment, reaching an enormous climax where the overlapping phrases return. Instead of ending in triumph, though, Berlioz closes with quiet, long-held notes and twilit harmony.

The second part, Tibi omnes Angeli—To You all angels cry—is subtitled Hymn. Following a long, quiet organ solo, the female chorus enters hesitantly, interrupted by the organ, strings, and winds. But when they arrive at the angels' cry of Sanctus—Holy—the high woodwinds add a repeated phase in unhurried sixteenth notes that depict tonally their fluttering wings. This builds to a climax for the full chorus and brass. The next iteration of Sanctus is accompanied by fast-moving pizzicatos in the strings alongside dissonant notes for the trumpets and trombones that add metallic gleam. Berlioz alternates verses praising God, Christ, apostles, martyrs, and prophets with his great setting of the Sanctus, the third and last of which is accompanied by a sharply rhythmic figure for the violins and violas. There's also a spacious and quiet postlude for the organ in dialogue with the strings and woodwinds.

The composer's footnote for the optional third movement instructs that it should not be performed except to celebrate a military victory.[47] Titled Praeludium, this three-minute orchestral interlude effectively sets a tone that's nobly reflective, rather than pompous or triumphant. The side drums tapping out a march rhythm that open the passage immediately strike a military pose. Skirling winds are joined by the heavy brass, with the strings then cooling things down. But the harmonies take unexpected, proto-modern turns; and after a brassy climax, as he so often does, Berlioz finds his way to a quiet closing.

The fourth part, Dignare, Domine—Grant, Lord—has the subtitle Prayer, and is, happily, mandatory. Opening with a quiet exchange for strings and organ that sets forth the penetrating rising interval of the primary melody, the small ensemble is soon joined by sighing figures for the flutes, clarinets, and horns. The soprano chorus takes the penetrating melody, which Berlioz treats in free counterpoint with the rest of the chorus joining, some fugally, others in murmured commentary. Meanwhile, the orchestral textures are thickening gradually, first with detached chords for the winds, then an exchange of falling figures between the high woodwinds and the violins. This inventive passage—Die isto sine peccato nos custodire—Keep us this day without sin—is notable too for the boldness and beauty of its ever-shifting harmonies. Keeping to a steady, moderate pace, Berlioz masterfully maintains the dreamlike tone established at the start. He builds to a climax at the center of the movement with one of those phrases relocated from another place in the text, Aeterna fac cum sanctis tuis—Let them be numbered with your saints—from which the music then retreats gradually, giving the section a symmetry that's not overly rigid as it falls gently and always beautifully to a quiet end.

The Hymn Christe, rex Gloriae—Christ, king of glory—opens unpromisingly as a loud and blustery fugue for the full chorus. But Berlioz has some surprises in store, reducing the volume, speed, and even the choral forces for Tu, ad liberandum—You who took it upon yourself—that's gently punctuated by the flutes and clarinets. His brilliant theme of long-held suspensions for the chorus over pizzicato strings from the Resurrexit of the Mass is resurrected here as a new setting for Tu ad dexteram Dei sedes—You, who sits at God's right hand. The fugue returns abruptly, now enriched by more sophisticated harmony and relieved by occasional drops in dynamics. Tu, ad dexteram also returns, this time accompanied by shuddering rather than plucked strings, all underpinned by a falling bass line that's far more sophisticated than its ancestor of 1824. The big chords that end the movement also take some unexpected harmonic turns.

Another descendant of the 1824 Mass, Te ergo quaesumus—We therefore pray—expands on the mournful melody of the Agnus Dei, which is initially presented intact, even holding to the same key. With this later treatment running about three minutes longer, Berlioz has more room to expand on the noble material. For example, a switch to the major key occurs only in the final moments of the Agnus Dei of the Mass. But here the change, which appears on the words Fiat super nos Misericordia tua, Domine—Have mercy on us, Lord—is longer and more clearly hopeful in tone. As before, it's set for a tenor, this work's only vocal soloist. And as before, he's joined by the female chorus, though much earlier along. This movement is also much more elaborately and richly scored, with notable contributions by the cornets and trombones adding a solemn, choralelike background.

The massive finale and capstone of the Te Deum is a huge movement of high purpose and dramatic impact. Berlioz cuts and shifts the text of the ancient hymn, joining two phrases, Judex crederis esse venturus—We believe you will come to be our judge—from about three-quarters of the way through with the closing words, In te, Domine, speravi, non confundar in aeternum—In you, Lord, I have trusted, let me never be confounded—along with a few other carefully selected lines. He repeats and exchanges these many times in a densely structured arch, in which counterpoint, his favorite 9/8 meter, and the work's most massive choral group are engaged. The children's chorus makes its last and most notable appearance here.

Titled Hymn and Prayer, this astonishing finale opens with a heavy-footed, marchlike theme for the organ that will dominate its entire structure. Strangely, it's set in the non-march-like 9/8 beat. The basses enter with a long subject that's treated in free counterpoint. Other choral elements join in a dark-hued battle into which a little light is allowed to penetrate in the form of a five-note falling phrase in the high woodwinds and violins, as Berlioz also changes the meter to 3/4, providing relief after the relentlessness of the 9/8 march. But he reintroduces the march quietly in several orchestral and vocal lines, with the children joining in tones as urgent and anxious as the adult choruses. The trudging march gradually resumes its dominance, leaving us unsure whether triumph is imminent or even possible. With an abrupt change of key, the reappearance of the five-note falling theme, trumpet fanfares, and some taps on the snare drum, victory seems to be at hand. But even here, the composer colors this fierce musical drama with powerful reiterations of the march for the chorus. Only in the final moments does he allow for resolution to the major key, a uniform 3/4 beat, and triumphant cries for the chorus. But, by then, they are so clouded that the victory feels hard-won, uncertain, and ambiguous.

The second of the two optional movements follows. "For the presentation of the colors" means it's background music for ceremonies in which the national and regimental flags are brought in and displayed. Nothing could differ more from the great spiritual battle that just ended than this dapper exercise in vamping, which is still attractive and interesting. It's notable too for the twelve harps Berlioz introduces into the orchestral texture halfway through. Deploying a march tune presented initially by the woodwinds and brass, he maintains a cool, serious tone to the end.

L'Enfance du Christ—The Childhood of Christ

A triumph at its premiere in 1854, this "sacred trilogy"—essentially a dramatic oratorio—remains one of Berlioz's most popular compositions, though like so much of his oeuvre it is rarely performed live. The work has an interesting genesis: the composer sketched what would turn into the "Shepherd's farewell" from the completed work's second part, as a bored guest at a Parisian card party in 1850. This he published under the fictional name of Pierre Ducré, improbably dated 1679. From this kernel, the work sprouted in sections, with part 2 (The Flight into Egypt) completed first, followed by part 3 (The Arrival at Saïs), and the first and for many listeners the best (Herod's Dream) last. As a result, the three parts don't cohere in style and mood.

Berlioz himself wrote the straightforward and effective text, which does, however, stray from its biblical roots in Matthew 2. The work is religious in thrust, but never showy and rarely even loud. The composer's sense of drama still comes through clearly in words, music, and structure. *L'Enfance du Christ* is built of ensembles, duets, and one of his greatest arias, O misère de rois—Sad lot of a king. As we'll see, the score gives location settings and even some stage directions to the singers and chorus. Is *L'Enfance du Christ* an opera on a biblical subject—there are many—or an oratorio? It's an oratorio; but, like Handel, Berlioz couldn't keep his operatic instincts from poking through.

By the time he composed *L'Enfance*, Berlioz was no longer a believer. But that did not keep him from writing one of the most marvelous sacred works. As his biographer and critic David Cairns explains, Berlioz created an idealized version of his hometown church's choir, recapturing his own youthful wonder at that sound. The score also has delicate tinting of folk music from eastern France and more sophisticated compositional techniques, including some early examples of orientalism, the Middle Eastern flavoring that became an obsession with composers over the next eighty years.[48] Berlioz's music may be sophisticated, but its effect is direct and pure, rendering the familiar story with the delicacy of a musical fairy tale. Flaws notwithstanding, *L'Enfance du Christ* may be his most lovable work. Perhaps only the *Christmas Oratorio* of

Heinrich Schütz (1660; and unlikely Berlioz knew it) is comparable in its simplicity of expression achieved by means of profound skills toward the same goal.

As the subtitle says, the "Sacred Trilogy" is set in three sections that in many ways resemble operatic acts. As noted, each part is subtitled and then further subdivided into scenes, each with a title. Vocalists take distinct parts: a soprano is the Virgin Mary, a baritone sings the role of her husband Joseph. The great role of Herod is sung by a bass. The Roman soldier Polydorus is also a bass; another soldier in part 1 is a tenor. A kindly Ishmaelite who takes the Holy Family in is a bass. So far, rather operatic. The last vocal part, that of a narrator, is sung by a tenor.

Part 1 ("Herod's Dream") opens with the most oratorio-like passage in *L'Enfance*, sung by the narrator, that describes Jesus's birth and the waves of disturbance and hope caused by that event. These words, in recitative, are accompanied by plain chords for the woodwinds. The Nocturnal March that follows is one of Berlioz's most wonderful character pieces, evoking the setting as described in the score (A street in Jerusalem. A small troop of soldiers on night-patrol) with delicacy. Clear-textured counterpoint is his primary means, with the complexity of that technique never threatening the magical mood of the music. Berlioz uses muted French horns and strings to darken orchestral timbres, and several rhythmic procedures, including syncopation, to vary the pulse, but, again, never violating the fine-boned nature of his rendering. The composer builds to a climax as transition to the next passage where Polydorus and another Roman soldier complain of life in the awful backwater of Jerusalem and of Herod, its crazed ruler. The score of *L'Enfance* is by now operatic, with settings, stage directions, and recitatives all marked clearly.

The wonderful march returns as postlude to their dialogue. The next scene consists of Herod's great lament. Set in a typical ABA form with a powerful introductory passage, the main melodic material (A) is reprised after a contrasting middle section. The form is typical of opera and sacred music, with most arias in Bach's cantatas and Passions set in the same way. The coiled, spinning figure for strings that opens the aria, reminiscent of Haydn or Beethoven, introduces Herod, who will act monstrously when he orders the massacre of all newborn children, but for whom Berlioz's music nevertheless creates pity. The aria proper begins with a tragic melody stated by the violas and cellos against a limping pizzicato figure for the other strings, and a parallel countermelody, usually taken by the bassoons and French horns.[49] Herod's phrases, echoed heavily by the orchestra, describe his misery and fear: Régner et ne pas vivre—To reign, but not to live. In the middle section, over somewhat lighter textures but still expressing desolation, he sings of his envy of the shepherd's simple life, then pleading in a wide-ranging vocal line with night to let him rest: A mon sein ravagé donne la paix une heure—Grant my anguished heart an hour of peace. The main melody returns, decorated by broken figures for the high woodwinds; a spacious postlude for the orchestra ends the section in a rare blend of grandeur and despondency.

Giuseppe Verdi and Berlioz knew and admired each other;[50] Verdi made it his business to study the Frenchman's scores. Verdi's Requiem is the best-known example of Berlioz as his inspiration. This aria may well have served as the model for another Verdian masterstroke: King Philip's aria, Ella giammai m'amo—She never loved me—from *Don Carlo*, composed and revised between 1866 and 1886. Their dramatic settings are identical: a sleepless, troubled monarch lamenting his isolation. Musically, one can hear similarities in the form, in their spaciousness and grandeur, as well as in details, including the prominent roles for the cello, and the difficult, far-ranging, but always expressive part for the singer. Verdi's aria is just as good as Berlioz's, which deserves to be better known.

A brief third scene consists of an encounter between Herod and Polydorus, who enters, startling the king. Soothsayers Herod had sent for are then introduced, to galumphing figures in the lower strings. To a barbaric-sounding harmony known as open fifths, forbidden academically to Western composers but a good example of the Berlioz's use of exotic coloring in *L'Enfance*, they ask Herod why he has called them. In a long recitative, accompanied by a mournful clarinet, he tells them of his insomnia and the recurring dream of the birth of a child destined to overthrow him. In the astonishing fast-tempo passage that follows, the Soothsayers dance, gesture, and consult to the accompaniment of a sinister melodic phrase, oscillations between major and minor harmonies, and thrumming strings in dizzying alternations of 3/4 and 4/4 meters, interrupted occasionally by a decisive rising gesture. Of unprecedented boldness in mainstream nineteenth-century music, this great passage is as strange and ominous as Berlioz intended. And it's not without an innocent charm, too.

To a spare, dark-hued accompaniment, the Soothsayers confirm the bad news. Their advice to have every newborn child killed is set to another major-minor oscillation, in which the plangent tone of the oboe dominates. Herod readily agrees, in a fierce, fast-moving concerted passage where he's joined by the Soothsayers, egging him on. A long, powerful orchestral postlude, featuring the heavy brass in their only appearance in this delicately scored work, suggests rather than depicts the slaughter of the innocents. Thundering away in rhythmic patterns that recall the Requiem, the composer evokes the awful event, ending with a slithering chromatic fall for the woodwinds.

The change of mood as the scene shifts to the stable in Bethlehem where the Holy Family is taking shelter is sharply drawn. The lyrical duet O mon cher fils—Oh, darling child—is set by Berlioz in a pastoral mode, with woodwinds dominating the accompaniment and the vocal lines of Mary and Joseph intertwining sweetly. Berlioz's text is an apostrophe to the infant, mostly from Mary, in which she advises him to take care of his sheep, a metaphor for mankind.

Alongside pulsing figures for the oboes, English horn, and clarinets, the primary melody is introduced by the flutes, violins, and a solo cello. In tranquil tones, Mary introduces Jesus to his metaphorical flock in a beautiful tune that shows Berlioz at his most poetic. The sheep's bleating is imitated throughout by the winds, and their tendency to caper and play is echoed by orchestral scampering. Joseph doesn't join until almost halfway through, but he echoes Mary at a sweet harmonic interval throughout. The coda—the closing passage—is as sweetly dreamy as that of Herod's furious scene was horrifying.

In the sixth and last scene of part 1, Mary and Joseph are warned by angels to flee Judea. Berlioz carefully differentiates mortal and divine creatures in this beautiful dialogue. The angels, always accompanied by an organ, sing from offstage at one slow tempo, to which Mary and Joseph reply with increasing animation as the awareness of their danger grows. While the angels sing in conventionally nineteenth-century angelic music, similar to Wagner's *Lohengrin*, Berlioz renders the high-set writing for the orchestra and celestial harmonies convincingly. The angels' closing word, Hosanna, is allowed to move a bit more freely and is orchestrated with rare delicacy, eloquently underlined by the cellos. The composer's instructions on how to soften the sound of the choral group singing as angels, which inevitably come through only vaguely in recordings, are astonishingly detailed. Berlioz instructs that they stand behind a curtain, then turn their backs to the audience.[51]

Part 2, "The Flight into Egypt," is set in three sections that are not labeled scenes, as in parts 1 and 3. The long overture that opens the section is meditative, polyphonic, and magical. Set for strings and a small group of woodwinds, the fugal subject stated initially by the violins has an open sound due to the insertion by Berlioz, carefully clarified in the score, of a tone that's not normally part of the key. The second iteration of the subject, given initially by the English horn, then the woodwinds, feels even more outdoorsy and fresh; rhythmic play for the flutes and later the English horn, and finally the full wind section, keeps the thematic treatment interesting and unpredictable. Technical explanations aren't needed to help listeners understand something so obviously beautiful. This movement clearly anticipates the sound of the Finnish symphonist Jean Sibelius.

The "Shepherd's farewell" that forms the second section of part 2 is the origin of *L'Enfance du Christ*, sketched by Berlioz at a card party. This gentle lullaby for oboes, clarinets, strings, and chorus is easy to grasp. Flawlessly executed, the movement opens with a musical push of the hand on the cradle in the form of accented chords for the woodwinds. This figure opens each of the three verses, occasionally punctuating the last verse as well. The chorus, accompanied by the strings, softly sing the lullaby Il s'en va loin de la terre—He [Jesus] must go far from here. Berlioz keeps what might turn sleepy interesting by staggering the entries of the chorus, and the harmonic background is quietly complex as well. As in life, the final verse, Cher enfant, Dieu te bénisse—Dear child, God bless you—is sung at the lowest volume, as the child finally dozes off, though here it's richly harmonized, too. A final twitch of the woodwinds closes this marvelous passage.

"The Holy Family resting at the wayside" forms the third portion of part 2. Half tone poem, half narrative, this passage resembles the overture in both lyrical tone and extraordinary beauty. A dialogue between the woodwinds and strings forms the first half, with the composer shifting the piercing melody freely between instruments and major and minor tonalities. The lilting 6/8 beat in which the plaintive tune is set also helps work its way quickly into the mind. Once the long melody has been fully treated by the orchestra, the narrator reappears, telling of the family's weariness and their delight at finding shade and fresh water at an oasis: Les pélerins étant venus—The pilgrims, having come. The tale of their exhaustion is related to much the same material as before with some minor adjustments for text-setting; we realize as well that some of the open freshness of the music was created to depict the cool water described by the narrator. The ending is astonishing, too, as angels appear to sing two slow, ecstatic Hallelujahs over the divine child.

Part 3, "The Arrival at Saïs," was the second to be completed, and is set in three scenes. Beginning with another strongly profiled, lightly scored, proto-Sibelian tune, the narrator relates the desperation of Mary and Joseph as they travel to Egypt, now without food, water, or possessions. Although almost as beautiful as the tunes in the first and third scenes of part 2, this has more impetus, helping move the singer through a fair amount of narration. Berlioz deploys a number of methods, including variation of the melody, rhythmic shifts, and compressions, and in the middle, when Mary is described: Seule Sainte Marie marchait—Only Mary walked—of folklike harmonies.

Mary begins the duet with choral interjections that follow, Dans cette ville immense—In this huge city—the masterful dramatic high point of part 3. Right away the high-set, broken phrases for the violas express the anxiety of Mary and Joseph, now not only hungry but frightened in an unfamiliar urban setting. Yet, for all its unmistakable urgency, the orchestral treatment never loses its delicacy, as when Joseph's timid knocking on unfriendly doors is rendered with light, rhythmic taps on the timpani, an instrument Berlioz understood better than most. Their pleas are met with rejection, energetically barked by the chorus.

Finally they are allowed in: Entrez, entrez, pauvres Hébreux—Come in, poor Hebrews—by a kindly Ishmaelite. This gentleman immediately sets his children and servants to help the Holy Family, which they do to a fine fugal bustle, starting with the chorus and slowing, on subtle shifts of rhythm, with the orchestra. In a dialogue in recitative between Joseph and the Ishmaelite, the latter comments amusingly that their child's name is charming, and after some bustling passages, the Ishmaelite learns that Joseph is a carpenter like himself and invites the poor Hebrews into the family business. The Ishmaelite calls for entertainment at the end of this long and difficult day. A trio for two flutes and harp that follows is, obviously, a lighter divertissement. Attractive in a quirky way, it's also one of the clearer displays of exoticism in *L'Enfance*.

Noticing that Mary is weeping with gratitude, the Ishmaelite sings a lullaby, Allez dormir, bon père, bien reposez—Go to sleep, good father, rest well—in which he, Mary, Joseph, and the chorus express their varied feelings of relief and sympathy. The composer builds the warm feeling of this ensemble with a sweet melody, harmonized with sophistication, accompanied by rocking strings and embroidered by the woodwinds.

The final section, titled Epilogue, opens with long-held notes widely separated in time. These, at first for violin and viola, then in connected but still very long notes for the woodwinds, take up about one minute of this passage's ten-minute duration. Resembling breathing, they stop all sense of forward motion and impose calm on the last moments of *L'Enfance du Christ*. The narrator, in recitative, concludes the history of the Holy Family up to their return to Judea, with Jesus grown La tendresse infinie à la sagesse unie—With infinite love and wisdom united. The closing pages are taken by an a capella, nearly motionless hymn for the chorus and narrator, O mon âme—Oh, my soul—in which the singers and narrator exchange praise of God. A great ending to a great work, the final chorus is not for the restless, needing time and patience to show its meanings and beauties. Some notes are held for so long that the chorus is instructed by Berlioz to breathe separately for the fully sustained delivery he wants. There's a final, carefully gauged diminuendo that makes the closing Amens seem to fade away.

Sacred Music, Part 2
The Requiem
(Grande Messe des morts)

Berlioz's Great Mass for the Dead—the Requiem—was commissioned in 1836 by the Ministry of the Interior. Its initial purpose, like that of the *Symphonie funèbre et triomphale*, was to honor the dead of the July 1830 Revolution. Following a series of setbacks possibly attributable to the composer's enemies, and certainly to the inertia of several ministers and ministries, the work was first performed on December 5, 1837, at the funeral service of a general killed in battle in Algeria.

In his autobiography, Berlioz writes with energy and humor about the trials and travails attending its commission and the first performance. Under ministerial pressure, the composer uneasily allowed François-Antoine Habeneck to conduct the premiere. The older Habeneck was no friend, if grudgingly respectful of Berlioz's avant-garde style. Vividly described but also most debated is Berlioz's charge that Habeneck put down his baton to take a pinch of snuff at the moment in score—the start of the Tuba mirum—where the conductor's direction in setting a new tempo is absolutely required.[52] The composer claims to have watched Habeneck in alarm, jumping up and signaling the new tempo himself, thus saving the day. Not everyone present noticed; there's speculation, too, that it happened at the dress rehearsal, leading some to doubt the composer's memory or his veracity. It's safe to say that today a plurality of historians accepts Berlioz's account. From then, Berlioz suspected Habeneck of acting on behalf of his various enemies to sabotage the performance.

Although his own religious belief was waning, the Requiem—which in its essence looks at how man faces the mystery and terror of death—

was a project Berlioz was eager to tackle. In this and, as we'll see, in other ways, he anticipates Verdi, another nonbeliever and profound musical dramatist who composed the other great liturgical Requiem of the nineteenth century. Berlioz wrote, "For a long time the text of the *Requiem* had been to me an object of envy, on which I flung myself with a kind of fury when it was put within my grasp."[53] As the rediscovery of the *Messe solennelle* of 1824 has shown, he recycled some impressive ideas, often in grander form, in the later work.[54] Aside from Luigi Cherubini, whose two Requiems didn't have much influence on Berlioz, those whose church music did (Méhul, Gossec, and his teacher Jean François Le Sueur[55]) are now little known, even inside the musical community. Verdi, who composed his Requiem in 1874, clearly knew Berlioz's well, profiting in a salutary way from his familiarity with the score. Wagner also benefited, admiring and imitating Berlioz's method of introducing bare melodies, without accompaniment or harmonization, that seem initially to float. Five of the Requiem's ten sections open this way. Mahler also admired Berlioz's dramatic sense and spaciousness, adapting some of his methods.

Long sections at the work's opening and closing are carefully balanced by breaks in mood and musical treatment within, and by shorter movements. The long sixth and seventh sections, the Lacrymosa and Offertorium, stand as its central pillars, complementing each other with their radically differing characters. Strange, singular, and terrifying, the Lacrymosa (Track 7) may be the Requiem's pinnacle and is indisputably one of the composer's greatest inspirations. Yet the Requiem has its flaws, with noble and powerful ideas sitting alongside lapses of taste and judgment. Although the entire work, as well as each section, is carefully structured, at times it seems to sprawl. As with most of Berlioz's oeuvre, repeated listening over time is essential to full appreciation; but to know it is almost certainly to love it.

All settings of the Catholic high Requiem Mass—"high" meaning one set to music—reflect the composer's individual goals and emphases. Berlioz divides his into ten sections:

1. Requiem et Kyrie
2. Dies irae

3. Quid sum miser
4. Rex tremendae
5. Quaerens me
6. Lacrymosa
7. Offertorium
8. Hostias
9. Sanctus
10. Agnus Dei

Berlioz's breakdown doesn't show further subdivisions or significant differences in their length and musical textures. For example, several (the opening and closing movements as well as the Dies irae, of which the Lacrymosa is actually the closing verse, the Offertorium, and Sanctus) each take ten to twelve minutes to play, assuming primary positions in the work, with the others running roughly half that length. While his Requiem is famous for its thunderous passages, there are probably more quiet moments that express fear, timid hope, or reflection.

Like Berlioz, Verdi made the Dies irae, parts 2 through 6 listed here, the centerpiece of his Mass. The text of this long passage, dating to the thirteenth century, depicts the terrors of the Day of Judgement. It's full of the morbid obsessions of a superstitious time. Both nineteenth-century masters take full advantage of the trumpets that will wake the dead (Tuba mirum) in passages of stupefying power and volume. Berlioz's enormous Lacrymosa is based on a limping theme cast in the composer's well-loved 9/8 meter. His Sanctus is an exceptionally sweet dialogue for women's chorus and a tenor, the only solo vocalist.

In his desire to cast the work as a cyclical musical drama, Berlioz shifted parts of the liturgical text around. The liturgy of the Mass is, essentially, its script, a text one would expect to be unalterable. But he moved phrases and even full verses around freely, omitting one prayer, the Benedictus, completely.[56] Doing so gave him control over the flow of the work, allowing him to change emphases at a word—which may have been one he himself moved there. Of the many examples of his influence on Verdi, none is more important. Following Berlioz's example, Verdi also shifted the text, turning liturgy into potent musical drama. On the musical side, whereas Berlioz returns to thematic material presented earlier in the final parts of his Mass, Verdi's conception is more deliberately cyclical. But their affective goals were different. Verdi ends his Requiem in terror and uncertainty, whereas Berlioz achieves a more peaceful conclusion.

> The numbers indicated are only relative. If space permits, the chorus may be doubled or tripled and the orchestra may be proportionately increased. But in the event of an exceptionally large chorus, say 700 to 800 voices, the entire chorus should only be used for the Dies irae, the Tuba mirum and the Lacrymosa, the rest of the movements being restricted to 400 voices.[57]

Perhaps most immediately striking about the Requiem is the startling number of singers and instrumentalists called for, with 391 specified in the score. As the composer's note about this shows, more can be accommodated, and are in fact welcome. Berlioz's basic requirement is for 210 choral singers, the tenor soloist, and 181 instrumental players.

Given the funereal subject of the work, Berlioz's orchestra is weighted toward low-pitched instruments, including eight bassoons and four tubas. He also calls for four brass ensembles, totaling thirty-eight players, to be placed around the main orchestra, designated in his layout to its North, East, South, and West, that is, to its sides, in front and behind. All consisting of heavy brass, these include a total of sixteen trombones and add another six tubas; they stand for the celestial trumpets that call the living and dead to judgment on the world's last day. Equally remarkable is the percussion section, led by eight pairs of timpani, with each drum tuned to a specified pitch. Contrary to what one might expect, they're rarely struck loudly, and there's probably no more extensive and subtle use in the repertory of this beautiful instrument than Berlioz's here. Also worth noting is the requirement for ten pairs of cymbals. It may seem comical, even mad, but the composer knew what he wanted, plotting his effects carefully.

The Requiem was commissioned with its first performance at the huge Church of the Invalides in Paris (the burial place of various Bonapartes, including Napoleons I and III, as well as other French military heroes). This fired the composer's sonic imagination; as we've seen, Berlioz already thought big. He appreciated the echo-laden interior as the setting for his vast musical-spiritual drama. A great 1975 performance led by Leonard Bernstein recorded at the Invalides shows that the church setting works and makes one wish to have been there. But the forces required for a live performance make the Requiem a rare visitor to either church or concert hall. When it is performed, curiosity about the size and makeup of the ensemble can obscure the work's qualities. Recordings have the benefit of allowing listeners to get to know the Requiem, but surely no home sound system can match the thing played live; I deeply regret not yet having heard it in person.

As the heading suggests, the opening Requiem and Kyrie is set in two broad sections. The first and longer part begins quietly with an ominous, unharmonized rising scale broken by long pauses, ending in a gloomy phrase for the woodwinds and strings. (Wagner's *Parsifal* opens with a similar phrase.) The chorus sings the first lines, Requiem aeternam dona eis, Domine—Grant them eternal rest, Lord—in tight canonic entries, starting with the basses, with tenors and sopranos joining in turn. A change to a major key and more fluid textures relieve the darkness just a bit; but soon the desolate opening returns, now louder and more insistent. There's another slight shift of tone as the male voices take up the next verse, Te decet hymnus—To you praise is due—in a pleading tone but a strange, bare harmony over a steadily moving figure for the cellos. The composer sets the tenors' line excruciatingly high, leading to audible straining he must have wanted. This isn't conventionally pleasing but, rather, deeply expressive.

A break from the severe counterpoint is finally allowed with the words Et lux perpetua luceat eis—And perpetual light shine upon them—as a soaring figure for the violins and a momentary shift to a major key remind us of the darkness in which we've persisted; the measures that follow return to tonal gloom, although beautifully. Berlioz brings back the rising violin figure again toward the end of the work.

The last prayer in the opening sequence of the Requiem sets the Greek language Kyrie eleison—Lord, have mercy—and Christe eleison—Christ, have mercy—that form part of the Catholic liturgy. Berlioz interprets the first in frightened whispering over plucked strings.

That to Christ as divine friend and intercessor is often (as in Verdi's) in a more hopeful tone contrasting with that to the stern Father. Berlioz minimizes the prayer to Jesus, changing to a more flowing phrasing, but always buried between Kyrie eleisons. At the end, these are compressed into a terrified entreaty over shuddering strings.

The long second part comprises the Dies irae—Day of wrath—and the Tuba mirum—The trumpet, spreading its wondrous sound—in a binary structure. Most composers—Mozart, Cherubini, and certainly Verdi—who have set this morbid text take advantage of its frightening qualities, writing music that grabs the listener immediately. Berlioz goes with a different approach, opening with eerie counterpoint that builds gradually over the first half of the section, giving the brassy eruption of the Tuba mirum fuller impact.

Made of carefully sculpted material, the Dies irae divides into three subsections. A somber, marchlike theme is stated, unharmonized, in the lower strings. The sopranos and high winds state a contrapuntal subject that's marked by pauses and limping rhythms. The basses, then tenors, enter in a fuguelike passage that gradually thickens in texture, while also building in volume. The strings comment with rising triplets that express a clearer sense of dread. With the next verse, Quantus tremor—What shuddering there will be—a new, tighter fugato begins. Dominated by the increasingly disturbing limping figure, sung by the tenors, and a striking countersubject (long-short-long-long) for sopranos and woodwinds, this section is even more oppressive. The ominous rising triplets in the strings introduce another iteration of the Quantus tremor verse and another fugal subject, more flowing but joined by the old ones in denser polyphony.

Having built our anticipation, Berlioz the musical dramatist delivers his big punch. (This is where Habeneck put down his baton.) The four brass bands, symbolizing the fearsome summons to judgment from the four corners of the earth, cut loose with loud fanfares after which the bass chorus comes in, with another uncomfortably high vocal line, Tuba mirum spargens sonum—The trumpet, spreading its wondrous sound—as the timpani enter thunderously. Berlioz staggers the entrances of the instrumental parts, making the beat hard to feel; the brass bands also play in different keys. The effect is wonderfully bewildering, as was surely his goal. Of course, neither singers, nor players, nor audience can take high volume for long, so the composer quiets down momentarily for the setting of the verse Mors stupebit—Death will be stupefied—also returning to a clear beat as the sopranos and tenors finally join the basses, momentarily the softening the stern texture. The fanfares resume with the next lines, Liber scriptus proferetur—A book will be brought forth—leading to a massive orchestral climax including the cymbals, making a stunning noise, and leading into the final section, Judex ergo cum sedebit—When the judge is seated. Berlioz artfully manages a quiet ending on broken phrases of text.

Here we see Berlioz as the great innovator who paved the way for Verdi and Mahler. He adds more brass instruments than the others and keeps them in the same performing space. The Tuba mirum of Verdi's Requiem also begins with muttered trumpet fanfares for two instruments on the platform and four offstage. This builds quickly to another passage of enormous power that runs three minutes to Berlioz's six. Whereas Berlioz stuns with massive sonorities, Verdi's vision is one of high velocity. For another clear example of influence, look to Mahler, who used Berlioz and Verdi as models in the finale of his Symphony No. 2, which addresses death and resurrection using a poetic rather than a liturgical text. There, he emulates Berlioz's spaciousness and Verdi's placement of brass instruments offstage. Neither Verdi nor Mahler are plagiarists; they are, like all artists, adapters of techniques and ideas learned from predecessors to their own material and for their own aesthetic goals.

Berlioz deploys a singular ensemble for the next verse, Quid sum miser tunc dicturus?—What am I, miserable one, then to say? The male chorus is accompanied by low strings, two English horns, and eight bassoons. This expression of desolation and humility moves at a steady, slow tempo and remains mostly at soft volume, a quiet valley between the Tuba mirum and the Rex tremendae that follows. The pleading melody that dominates this short movement is heard in the woodwinds right at the start, echoed in a gloomy and compressed reply by the strings below. Tenors sing the text in broken phrases, interrupted regularly by a two-note sigh for the English horns. The volume is increased just a little for the closing line, Gere curam mei finis—Take care of me at the end—in which the basses finally join. Although not the most attention-grabbing section of the Requiem, the Quid sum miser is effective, holding up well on repeated hearing.

The prayers that follow change in tone, leading Berlioz to attempt a more literal treatment, but the result is abrupt and chaotic. As it does for most other composers, the opening line, Rex tremendae majestatis—King of fearful majesty—dictates the awestruck nature of its setting. Returning to a full orchestra with brass bands and chorus, Berlioz opens with loud chords from the woodwinds and cries from the chorus, followed by a hearty tune that jogs upward, answered with the kind of foursquare reply he usually avoids. The rising phrase for the next line, Qui salvandos salvas gratis—Who freely saves the redeemed—receives delicate contrapuntal treatment and attractive instrumentation, as well. Accelerations on Recordare, Jesu pie—Remember, merciful Jesus—don't suit the earnest nature of the words, culminating in Berlioz's greatest misjudgment, a bizarrely cheerful setting of Confutatis maledictis—Silencing the accursed. The return of the rising phrase for Qui salvandos, now set against pulsating woodwinds is welcome. Amid the excited outcries, the composer works in a subtle harmonic drop that suggests uncertainty, and navigates to a welcome, quiet ending.

Quaerens me, sedisti lassus—Seeking me, you sat down, exhausted—is, like Quid sum miser, another quiet passage in contrast with those before and following. This is set for the unaccompanied choir, the familiar musical term for which is *a capella*. While a competent polyphonic display, it seems a bit less fine than Quid sum miser. The clashing entries at the words Ingemisco, tanquam reas—I sigh as one accused—reflect the text delicately, but the basses bumpy four-note contribution beginning at Preces meae non sunt dignae—My prayers are not worthy—seem out of kilter with the flowing lines of the other voices.

The Dies irae ends with one of the greatest sections of this Requiem, Lacrymosa dies illa—That tearful day. Berlioz really stretches out here, taking ten or more minutes to dramatize its sixteen words. The Lacrymosa is built of three thematic groups, with the powerful opening parts returning with even greater force to end the section. Complex from a musical standpoint, its meter is the 9/8 that Berlioz liked so well, but which he treats differently here.

Sacred Music, Part 2

In music, the beat is the rhythm that guides the music. Two familiar examples are marches, which are in 4/4 time, meaning each bar contains four quarter note beats. Waltzes, along with many other dances, are set in 3/4 time. To keep technical explanations to a minimum, 9/8 can be heard as an expansion of 3/4 time, with three strong beats (the first, fourth, and seventh of the nine) per bar, and, typically, a dancelike feel. Here, however, Berlioz roughs the beat up, making it lurch and stumble. As most have understood, his goal was to compose a "dance of death," a conceit dating back to the Middle Ages. More familiar in the visual arts than music, its moral is that all, from powerful to the poorest, are led in a metaphorical dance to the same end. The composer also manages to do justice to the text, even though weeping, rather than dancing, is its main trope.

Berlioz presents his themes, deeply original and strange, in the first moments, repeating them many times. Underlying the broad sections in which the Lacrymosa is cast are contrasting thematic strata, beginning with a scooping figure for the lower strings. There's a three-note outcry for woodwinds, and a big, slashing chord for the violins and violas. The composer gives the strings' chord prominence by placing it unexpectedly on a weak beat to startling and disturbing effect; giving the impression of the crack of a fearful whip. This is followed immediately by a powerful tone for twelve French horns. The chorus joins almost immediately, with an irregular, falling melody that contrasts with the jerky dance of the orchestra. Almost immediately, there are more painful high notes for the tenors, straining that can easily be heard in recordings with professional, normally rich-sounding choral groups. The altos, basses, and sopranos join in dense counterpoint.

With so short a text and everything fairly uniform thematically, textures need to be changed occasionally. In the second section, Berlioz lowers the volume and shifts the accompaniment to steadily pulsing strings. Accompanied by the bassoons and low strings, the basses growl along in commentary. He places the prayer to Christ, Pie Jesu Domine, dona eis requiem—Merciful Lord Jesus, grant them rest—at the quiet heart of this ferocious movement, setting it in detached notes for the basses as the rest of the chorus sings in longer lines, decorated with a gentle descant by the violins.

In the climactic second half of the Lacrymosa, Berlioz reprises all his material, but elaborated and with greater power. The return of the opening is accompanied by roars from the four brass bands and rumbling timpani; a falling melodic interval for the chorus from the pulsing second part is echoed emphatically by woodwinds. He builds thematic incarnations into climax upon climax. There's a dance that breaks into a clear beat, but fearfully heavy footed, followed by a shocking harmonic shift, and another mighty wave set to a rich-sounding harmonic technique known as suspensions. The composer's final inspirations are emphatic pounding on the bass drum that may symbolize dance or the terrified beating of the human heart. We hear the diminuendo—lowering of volume—on the final chord as inevitable.

Following his well-established principle of contrast, Berlioz sets the next section, the Offertorium—Offertory, a prayer to Jesus—with a quiet austerity. There's much to admire here, with the chorus limited until the final moments entirely to two notes (A-natural and B-flat) as the orchestra weaves an increasingly elaborate fabric alongside. A sense of mystery pervades this beautiful prayer. Unlike the Lacrymosa, the Offertorium also moves at an even pace, with the feeling of increasing motion coming from the composer's careful introduction of shorter note values into its textures.

The section begins with a rising theme in the violins and the chorus intoning its prayer, Domine Jesu Christe—Lord Jesus Christ—in broken phrases of three or five notes, punctuated by single note interjections for the woodwinds. Soon the rising tune is treated contrapuntally, with increasing motion. A stabbing phrase for the violins alternating with a swirling figure for flutes, oboes, and clarinets swells into an opulent melody alongside the words Libera animas omnium fidelium defunctorum de poenis—free the souls of all the faithful dead from punishment—that briefly colors without breaking the mood of delicate mystery. The chorus's timid interjections sometimes seem a world apart from the orchestra's activity, but as the section progresses, their harmonic and polyphonic connections grow clearer. The opulent violin melody is given a longer run over a pulsing accompaniment for the second violins and violas, then thinned to a single, lonely phrase for the first violins, the unlikely source of the movement's big climax on the phrase Libera eas, et sanctus Michael signifer repraesentet eas in lucem sanctam—Deliver them, and may the standard-bearer St. Michael bring them into holy light. (Michael, along with Gabriel, Raphael, and the less well-known Uriel, is one of the four archangels.) The opening melody is reprised by the string section under throbbing triplets for the winds. Again, the composer reduces the textures, finally allowing the chorus to break out into richly harmonized Amens.

The next part, Hostias—Sacrifices—is well known for widely separated chords for flutes and trombones, a striking effect that suggests aurally the gap between heaven and hell. Berlioz repeats the chords eight times over the course of the short (three and a half–minute) section. It has been shown that they serve a structural purpose here and in the closing Agnus Dei, where they return.[58] Whether they work aesthetically is another question. Amid this otherwise well-made prayer, their placement always seems random, and by the eighth iteration the growling trombones sound unintentionally comical. There's an honest chord for the strings to begin, a flowing nine-note figure, also for strings, that adds a bit of welcome momentum, and well-phrased, even affecting setting of the text for the male chorus.

Berlioz's influence on Verdi's Requiem can be heard clearly again in the opening moments of the penultimate section, the Sanctus—Holy. After a floated phrase for the violins that introduces the primary melody, this Requiem's only soloist, a tenor, sings a sweet, nearly motionless phrase over trembling violas and four muted violins. (Although Verdi sets his ecstatic tenor over trembling strings in the preceding Hostias, the example of Berlioz is obvious.) The female chorus replies softly to the tenor, whose tune soon reaches higher and into shifting harmonies in an unhurried expression of adoration. After the soloist sings a long-limbed, high-set line, Pleni sunt coeli et terra Gloria tua—Heaven and earth are filled with your glory—the chorus does not reply. Instead, they launch into a sturdy fugue, Hosanna in excelsis—Hosanna in the highest—which the composer instructs in the score to be sung "without violence," and which he brings to a quiet ending.

The opening Sanctus returns, its fervent stillness now contrasted with the busy fugue. In one of Berlioz's less conspicuous but still daring inspirations, the melody is decorated by the ten cymbals, softly struck, and quiet pulsing of the bass drum in an unusual counter-rhythm, as a solo flute also hovers above.[59] The fugue on Hosanna returns, much amplified by the orchestra, and brought now to a triumphant conclusion.

The final prayer of the Requiem, Agnus Dei—Lamb of God—another plea for peace, is a long movement cast in three broad sections. Berlioz brings back thematic material and text from earlier parts of the Mass, giving the work a cyclical feel and, again, pointing the way for Verdi, whose Requiem also revisits previous text and music with great effectiveness and power. Berlioz's closing consists of new material that's exceptionally beautiful.

Six quiet chords, for alternating woodwinds and strings, opens the section in a meditative mood. The male chorus begins the prayer, Agnus Dei, qui tollis peccata mundi, dona eis requiem sempiternam—Lamb of God, who removes the sins of the world, grant them everlasting rest—in phrases broken eight times (again) by the chords for flutes and trombones from the Sanctus. After a long pause, the six meditative chords that opened the section return, along with a figure for the strings that rises, then falls, signaling a change in pacing. The tenors take up the stern strains of the Te decet hymnus from the Requiem aeternam that opened the Mass. As before, the composer mellows the harmony as other groups of the chorus enter. To avoid monotony, Berlioz changes texture and pacing occasionally, allowing himself the opportunity for more delicate word setting. The radiant rising figure for violins from the opening is brought back just before the composer prepares for the magical closing passage, where his effects are, however, achieved with relative simplicity.

The timpani are reintroduced very softly to accompany the words Cum sanctis tuis in aeternum—With your saints in eternity—amid an otherwise thin accompaniment. With Quia pius es—Because you are merciful—the timpani pulse out a six-note figure. The strings, starting with the double basses, move up, then down again six times in broken chords forming a solemn harmonic rainbow. Each rising arch roams further from the key in which the work will end, with the falling side always outlining the home tonality. Each arch is accompanied by the drums' quiet pulsing, as the full chorus intones six final Amens. The closing of this extraordinary and sublime work consists of three soft notes for the strings and timpani.

Dramatic One-offs
Cléopâtre, Lélio, and Benvenuto Cellini

The three works in this chapter have nothing in common except that they are dramatically conceived and good enough that they merit hearing. Most significant by far is the opera *Benvenuto Cellini*, but the early cantata *Cléopâtre* is fine from start to finish. Least effective overall but still interesting is the curious assemblage that is *Lélio*, described by Berlioz as a *monodrame lyrique*—lyric monodrama—the six musical parts of which are introduced and linked by a narrator. The quality of its musical sections varies widely, and it's the most problematic of the three.

Cléopâtre

Sometimes referred to as *La Mort de Cléopâtre*—The Death of . . . , this work for soprano and orchestra is flawed but worth a hearing or two. Berlioz wrote it as his submission for the 1829 for the Prix de Rome, the competition he lost before winning the next year. The required work was a cantata, a generic term for a composition that's sung (from *cantare* in Italian) rather than played on instruments. J. S. Bach (1685–1750) is the most famous composer of cantatas, with the majority of his works in the form being religious. As Bach's dates tell you, the cantata was old and a bit tired by the time Berlioz found himself stuck with the job of writing one. But though green, he turned the onerous assignment into an opportunity. It's an impressive effort from the young composer. Its chief handicap is the absurdly wordy text by the playwright P. A. Viellard.

Broken into two sections, the second, subtitled *Méditation*—no translation necessary—is the more daring and powerful. But the fierce introduction for strings immediately grabs one's attention, and even though setting the verbose first verse is a challenge to Berlioz, he finds a tone of nobility for this musical and dramatic ancestor of Didon that carries through her entire monologue. The nostalgic second verse, Ah! Qu'ils sont loin ces jours—Ah, how distant are the days—suggests a warmer, more lyrical affect, to which Berlioz responds with a long-limbed melody over shifting harmonies that dominate the first half. Cléopâtre reflects on her triumphs and those of her ancestors. Opening with a somber, darkly scored chorale for the full orchestra, the Méditation is musically impressive from start to finish. Over a steady beat but in long, irregular phrases Cléopâtre confesses her unworthiness to the pharaohs—Grands Pharaons—whose mighty memories she has shamed. At the end, to a setting that vividly depicts her self-hatred, she sings that un vil reptil—a vile reptile—is now her only recourse. A sharply rising phrase for violins depicts the asp's sting. In the closing verse (Dieux de Nil—Gods of the Nile), feeling the effects of its poison, she sings in diminished voice and broken phrases over pulsing lower strings, then fades away. Berlioz's instrumental postlude is remarkable for its freedom, originality and power.

Lélio, ou Le Retour à la vie

Although Berlioz was gifted with irony and sharp sense of humor, these qualities abandoned him in the premise and structure of *Lélio, ou Le Retour à la vie*—Lélio, or the Return to Life, a pastiche of six numbers that the composer wanted to find a home for. He tried to bind these random items with a wordy narration that hasn't aged well. As one might expect, the music is very uneven, ranging from passable to almost great, with the best number, a tone poem for chorus and orchestra inspired by Shakespeare's *The Tempest*, saved for last. Berlioz's instruction at the start of the score that the work should be performed immediately following the *Symphonie fantastique*[60] feels cynical; and that everyone but the actor playing Lélio be hidden behind a curtain until the final number

Dramatic One-offs

downright odd. Lélio, clearly Berlioz himself on a grouchy day, praises Shakespeare in several of the narrations but also does an inordinate amount of complaining, which reaches a climax in the five-minute mega-kvetch preceding the final number. These narrations can and here will be summarized briefly.

The opening one, Dieu! Je vis encore—My God, I'm still alive—sets up the work with the assertion that the sensitive artist who murdered his beloved, had his head chopped off and witnessed the Witches' Sabbath that make up the last two movements of the *Symphonie fantastique* isn't really dead. Instead, this persona will narrate the rest; a misjudgment that trivializes the earlier work. He introduces a pretty, somewhat pale setting of a six-verse ballad by Goethe, Le Pêcheur—The Fisherman—for tenor accompanied by piano, which Lélio unwelcomely interrupts three times, and the supposedly hidden orchestra quietly intones the earlier work's motto-theme. Lélio-Berlioz's second monologue deals with his admiration for Shakespeare; leading him finally to introduce a beautiful and beautifully scored Choeur d'ombres—Chorus of shades (meaning ghosts)—for chorus and orchestra that clearly echoes Mozart's *Don Giovanni*, but not Shakespeare.

The next monologue continues with Shakespeare before turning to how hard it is for a young genius (guess who) to find appreciation. Turning clumsily to Italy, the Chanson de Brigands—Brigands' Song (J'aurais cent ans à vivre encore—Had I a hundred years to live), is introduced. Set in alternating verses for a baritone as their captain and an all-male chorus, this fine, angular number is better musically than its text, filled with the composer's signature rhythmic compressions, and interesting harmonic shifts that carry through from start to finish.

In the next spoken introduction, Lélio takes a long time to describe his gradually calming state of mind. This allows him to introduce the Chanson de Bonheur—Song of Bliss—for tenor. The glorious opening phrases breathe a Beethoven-like grandeur and calm, but the rest, set mostly for flutes, harp, and voice doesn't fulfill its promise. Lélio's next monologue serves to introduce a short orchestral passage, La Harpe éolienne, souvenirs—The Aeolian Harp, memories—referring to a mythological harp that was supposedly played by the winds. As it moves at a slow tempo, set (as you might expect) for harp and a trembling string orchestra, a solo clarinet adds its voice in this understated yet magical concerted piece.

Next, in a ridiculously long rant, Lélio promises that he will live for art before returning to Shakespeare again as a way to introduce the final musical number, the Fantaisie sur la Tempête de Shakespeare—Fantasia on Shakespeare's "The Tempest"—for orchestra and chorus. The longest and best section of *Lélio*, this complex overture-scherzo was written and performed twice in Paris in 1830, before the *Symphonie fantastique*, but political turmoil and bad weather kept audiences away.[61] Although far from perfect, it includes much beautiful material, keeping it interesting and easy to like.

Set for a full orchestra, chorus without basses representing the spirits of the air, and four-hand piano (two pianists playing one instrument), the work consists of four linked sections. First comes a prologue in which the magical mood of the island where Prospero and his daughter Miranda live. This is followed by the storm, then the action of the drama and a closing passage that recapitulates the opening. The text, curiously in "rudimentary Italian, presumably Berlioz's"[62] is not from the Shakespearean source but instead consists of a few evocative words, mostly calling Miranda's name; an odd and distracting weakness. But the delicately shifting harmony set to arpeggios and trills for the piano, suggesting waves lapping gently on the shore of the island where the play is set, instantly creates a magical mood. The chorus calls Miranda's name then sings that she will soon know love. The second section begins quietly, with fascinating irregular patterns in the strings and repeated taps on the bass drum that Berlioz develops into a powerful passage depicting the storm for the full orchestra; this is broken by a return to the opening themes.

The third section, depicting the action of the drama, opens with a phrase in light polyphony for the strings that suggests articulate dialogue as well as any music that isn't actual word-setting can; better than a comparable passage from the *Roi Lear* overture (see page 28). It soon shifts into a different meter and a more active mood as the chorus returns, again calling Miranda. A new thumping idea for low brass and strings summons a completely different character, which the chorus soon confirms, naming Caliban, orrido mostro—Caliban, horrid mon-

Dramatic One-offs

ster, Prospero's "savage and deformed slave"[63] from the play. His musical depiction, while vivid, is brief and the composer continues with his eloquent depiction of a drama that will end happily. The opening ideas return, along with more counsel and a farewell by the spirit-chorus to Miranda. The closing passage is a march in ever-accelerating tempos that's perhaps a bit more emphatic than necessary. *Lélio* is the most awkward frame imaginable for an interesting composition like the Tempest Fantasia: although the forces it requires are a bit unusual, it should be set free and performed on its own. Lélio gets the last word (Assez pour aujourd'hui—That will do for today), which at least this time is brief. The violins gently exhale the motto theme of the *Symphonie fantastique* again.

Benvenuto Cellini

Like its companions in this chapter, *Benvenuto Cellini* is hard to categorize. Berlioz subtitled it *opéra-comique*, so though not a tragedy, it's no comedy for Pompeo, who is killed by Cellini toward the end of act 1. Even the term *opéra comique* has multiple meanings, dating back to the separation of lighter dance-based entertainments originally performed in the streets from more noble tragedies that were sung in royal and aristocratic courts. It also became the name of a Parisian theater where these were performed, popular but second in prestige to the conservative and hide-bound Paris Opéra. Ironically, despite its subtitle this earliest and most daring of the composer's three operas had its premiere at that theater in September 1838 where, while "not the abysmal failure many writers have made it out to be . . . it was far from a rousing success."[64] The perpetual contrarian and underdog Berlioz found himself so in opposition to authority that even *Les Troyens*, his mature masterpiece and as noble as they come, was first performed at L'Opéra-Comique.

Be that as it may, anyone listening to *Benvenuto Cellini* will perceive that while comedy dominates its moods, it also contains enough romance and conflict to call it a drama, with some swashbuckling adventure thrown in. It was partially a romanticized self-portrait; the composer admired and clearly identified with the title character and youthful genius whose rough and roguish sides appealed to him, too. Berlioz lent a few of his own traits as a man and artist to his far-from-heroic protagonist. Like the Cellini of *Benvenuto Cellini*, Berlioz was paranoid about and scornful of his rivals and critics. The climactic casting scene that concludes the opera is not unlike the rehearsal or premiere of a new musical work, where creators must improvise solutions for a wide range of problems, like difficult material and unhappy personnel. Perhaps most telling is how the composer has Cellini put earlier works to new and better use. Cellini does this literally, sacrificing masterpieces from his studio for smelting into the great statue of Perseus, idealizing and dramatizing Berlioz's custom of recycling his own thematic material; hardly the same thing as destroying it.

The action-packed libretto by Léon de Wailly and Auguste Barbier is a free adaptation of the autobiography of Benvenuto Cellini (1500–1571), the great sculptor whose *Perseus* is on display in the Loggia de' Lanzi in the Piazza della Signoria in Florence. Other characters in Berlioz's opera, notably Ascanio and Balducci, appear in Cellini's book.

The virtuoso score was far too difficult for the instrumentalists and singers of the day, however, and remains to some "over-rich for the opera house."[65] The care Berlioz lavished on every passage of this beautiful mess will be obvious as you listen to this great but overstuffed music-drama, which languishes in semiobscurity. Certainly it influenced Wagner and Verdi, both of whom knew and admired Berlioz. The song of the metalworkers and apprentices and the riot in scene 2 clearly anticipates acts 2 and 3 of Wagner's *Die Meistersinger von Nürnberg*. Assuming that Verdi studied *Benvenuto Celllini*—and one must assume that he did—the weightless scampering in scherzolike passages for the lovers in act 1, scene 1 echo in *Falstaff*, his final operatic comedy.

Another difficulty stems from the fact that there is no definitive score for the opera either by Berlioz or assembled later by musicologists, making any production as much a scholarly as a musical project. The score has come down in three versions: "Paris 1" and "Paris 2," both from 1838; the three-act "Weimar" of 1852 was produced under the supervision of Franz Liszt in Germany.[66] But recordings don't match any of these exactly, and the rarity of live performances surely derives in part from this textual obstacle. Here, we'll follow the Colin Davis–led

1972 performance with Nicolai Gedda in the title role, as it's widely available and very fine; like everyone, Davis came up with his own version. (Don't be surprised to hear the passages in spoken dialogue, part of "Paris 1.") Those who find *Cellini* irresistible should also listen to the 2004 recording under John Nelson, also a hybrid but which includes a recorded appendix of omitted scenes.

Each of its two acts are further divided into two "tableaux," a word with multiple meanings in French that here denotes the physical setting for a scene. Act 1 consists of the first and second tableaux; act 2 has tableaux 3 and 4. Laden with twists and turns, *Benvenuto Cellini* takes place in sixteenth-century Rome during Holy Week.

Every bit as great as the *Carnaval romain*, *Corsaire*, and that of *Béatrice et Bénédict*, the self-contained overture has found a life of its own as a separate work, which you might think would stimulate an appetite for more of *Benvenuto Cellini*. Opening with a great swaggering gesture that depicts the artist-hero, this idea returns with even more energy later in the overture. The rest is a potpourri of themes from the work of contrasting character, including the solemn one in long notes from the pope's act 2 monologue in Cellini's studio, other material from the carnival scene in act 1, and a sweet tune from the duet for Cellini and Teresa in act 1, all orchestrated with stunning brilliance and in the composer's best manner, filled with startling rhythmic eruptions and harmonic shocks.

Act 1 opens with a complaint by the papal treasurer, Balducci, about a late-evening summons from the pope. His daughter Teresa is looking expectantly out the window. Outside, Cellini and a chorus are celebrating the start of Holy Week—Tra la la la . . . Carnaval père enterre ce soir un de ses fils—Tra la la . . . the Carnival king tonight is burying one of his sons. Teresa giggles as Balducci, who has been pelted with flour by the crowd, returns, grumbling and the merrymakers sing from offstage in an elaborate but lively ensemble that demonstrates from the get-go the complexities of music and stage action in *Benvenuto Cellini*. After Balducci leaves, Teresa sings her first aria, Entre l'amour et le devoir—Torn between love and duty—in which she delicately laments the conflict between her passion for Cellini and sense of responsibility to her father. In the opening passage, set at a moderate tempo, her melody is introduced by a solo oboe, to a pulsing string accompaniment. The music for this part of the aria, with the oboe adding more commentary, remains sweet and restrained, reflecting her youth and innocence. The second, faster portion, Quand j'aurai votre âge, mes chers parents—When I'm as old as you, my dear parents—takes a completely different tone. With its chirping melody in a stiff rhythm backed by gurgling winds and harp, Teresa looks ahead satirically to a time when love won't matter: Malheur à l'amour—To hell with love. Her aria ends with the kind of showy vocalism Berlioz despised but included here before he had the confidence and prestige to exclude cadenzas like this.

Cellini, then Fieramosca, enter, the latter bearing flowers. Note how Berlioz colors Cellini's tiny phrase C'est le gai carnaval qui dehors parle en mâitre—It's the Carnival, proclaiming its summons outside—with a festive shake of the tambourine. The three embark on a lengthy trio, known by Cellini's opening phrase, Ô Teresa, vous que j'aime plus que ma vie—O Teresa, you whom I love more than my life. She responds that she's forbidden to see him, in a high-set vocal line that's passionate but always lyrical. Fieramosca sings that sneaking and spying, marchant à pas de loup—creeping like a wolf—is a better way to win this girl's heart as the orchestra illustrates his method with stealthily plucked strings. Both lovers despise him, with their disgust expressed in wider ranging phrases and snarling trills for the strings, serving as a middle section for the trio. The opening is brought back, exquisitely reharmonized and laden with high notes for Teresa and Cellini. In the quick-tempo second portion of the trio, Ah! mourir, chère belle—What! death my love—Teresa and Cellini plot their escape to Florence in low voices and breathtakingly fast patter as Fieramosca catches and repeats a word here and there, though he finally grasps their scheme. The fine-boned scampering accompaniment for strings and winds makes a flawless background for what must be some of the most difficult singing in the repertory, though the composer works in a few slower, less demanding moments as when Teresa asks the Virgin Mary for forgiveness: Mère de tendresse, Vierge que sans cesse j'implore à genoux—Tender mother, Virgin to whom I kneel unceasingly in supplication. But the trio ends in faster, denser, quieter phrases: À demian soir—Till tomorrow evening.

In a spoken passage, Balducci enters Teresa's bedroom where neither Cellini nor Fieramosca are supposed to be. Cellini slips away, leaving Fieramosca to face Balducci's anger, which a short but vigorous chorus of neighbors joins: Ah! Maître drôle, ah! Libertin! Nous allons t'apprendre, suborneur—Ah, you rogue, you libertine! We'll teach you, seducer! The closing of this standard ensemble in nineteenth-century opera is enriched by the composer's rhythmic and harmonic energy.

Scene 2, set on Mardi gras—Fat Tuesday—before the start of Lenten fasting, is one of the two climactic scenes in *Benvenuto Cellini*. The second, which some feel is a bit of a letdown after the energy and force shown here,[67] is the opera's final scene, where the statue is cast. This scene, set in Rome's Piazza Colonna, also contains the material from which Berlioz drew the material for the *Carnaval romain* overture. Although it will end wildly, it opens with a romance—a lyrical aria of two verses—where Cellini describes the love for Teresa that has supplanted the thirst for greatness that once ruled him. Cellini's sentiment, La gloire était ma seul idole—Fame was my only god—is expressed tenderly from the start, punctuated by plucked strings and high woodwinds; the warmth and calm of the refrain, Protège-la, protège moi—Protect her, protect me—is backed by prayerful string chords demonstrating the change love has supposedly made to this fiery artist's outlook. In the second verse, he expresses gratitude that Teresa is willing to share: Ma vie errante et ma misère—My wandering and troubled life.

Cellini's assistants and apprentices enter, calling for wine, which is brought. Loosening up, Bernardino (one of the crew) calls for a song. Cellini agrees, but instructs that it should be a hymn to the glory of their craft. Their Chant des Ciseleurs—Song of the Metalworkers—is considered "the opera's philosophical centerpiece and one of the strongest scenes in the literature."[68] Initially setting it in energetic, angular phrases that reflect the rough and ready qualities of the workers (and that would make Beethoven proud), the composer adapts and develops the rhythmic accompaniment as they drink and grow unsteady. The initial verses, alternating with the chorus, ending with the words Honneur aux maîtres ciseleurs—Hail to the metalworkers—lists the treasures from under the surface of the earth: L'or comme le soleil luit, le rubis étincelle—Gold that gleams like the sun, sparkling rubies—and much more. The orchestra depicts their words in tone, with cymbals quietly echoing the metals they name and piccolos and flutes brightly accenting their list. Bernardino calls for more wine, but the whining innkeeper says the bill must be paid first, comically enumerating the bottles: Vin mousseux d'Asti, vin de Lipari, Lachryma-Christi, ce qui fait cent-trente—Sparkling Asti, wine from Lipari, Lachryma-Christi, that makes one hundred thirty. Without cash, Cellini and crew cry out in despair, but the day is saved by the entrance of Ascanio, his apprentice, with a payment from the pope for the still unfinished statue. Sung by a mezzo-soprano, Ascanio also brings a stern warning from the pope, who wants to see results from Cellini.

In his aria Cette somme t'est due—You are owed this money—Ascanio, accompanied by the metalworkers in chorus, explains that he had to get a promise from Cellini that the statue would be cast tomorrow. As strange as it can be and sounding only like Berlioz, the oath from Cellini and the workers is roared out earnestly, accompanied by gurgling high woodwinds. His conscience clear, Ascanio hands the money to Cellini, who in turn passes it to the innkeeper after complaining how little was sent. Blaming Balducci for the stingy installment, Cellini and the others plot to humiliate him in one of the pantomimes to be performed by their friend Cassandro and his troupe at the Carnival. The chorus curses Balducci in a refrain of the metalworkers' chorus.

Pompeo, a swordsman and friend of Fieramosca's, enters, and the two have a discussion in dialogue. Fieramosca now knows the full extent of Cellini's plots. He complains to Pompeo, who offers to help scotch the plans to escape with Teresa. Then, in a quick-moving comic aria, Ah, qui pourrait me résister—Ah, who can stand up to me—Fieramosca struts foolishly, calling himself a great swordfighter, declaring his love for Teresa, then pretending to duel: Un, deux, trois . . . Sans pitié je perce son coeur . . . Je suis vainqueur!—One, two, three . . . Pitilessly I run him through the heart. I am the victor! The orchestra mocks him with military fanfares as he threatens to make war, then tracks in subtle shifts of meter as he pretends to fence and stab his imaginary opponent. Although without sympathy for its object this musical caricature is remarkable for its richly varied textures, all to depict Fieramosca's movements and changing points of view.

Set in Rome's Piazza Colonna, the finale of act 1 is the great Carnival scene. The proto-cinematic opening seems to approach from afar, with thematic fragments and gradually increasing dynamics. It's also marked by brass fanfares that summon the revelers to the theater where Cellini's mockery of Balducci will take place. Balducci and Teresa enter, he commenting that it's beneath his dignity to watch this farce grossière—boorish farce—while she frets to herself about leaving her old father alone. Cellini and Ascanio, dressed as monks, sing delicately to each other that prudence et mystère—prudence and secrecy—are needed now. All the material the principals have been singing is joined in a brief but beautiful ensemble.

Brass fanfares, now fully phrased, open the main body of the scene, as actors and Roman citizens join in a high-energy chorus that climaxes with the words Ah, sonnez trompettes—Let the trumpets ring out. If you've listened to the *Carnaval romain* overture, you'll recognize this driving tune as its main theme; it's also very fast and hard to sing. More fanfares now quiet the crowd, which oohs and aahs at Cassandro's show, a pantomime that features the pope and someone who looks a lot like Balducci. Teresa wants to leave, but her father says he will stay to tell the pope: Comme on nous drape, et comme on sape notre pouvoir—How we're mocked and our authority undermined. The satirical pantomime continues with the audience calling for silence as harp and English horn carry the action with a beautiful, extended instrumental duet. The audience murmurs its approval. Then another player mimes as a morceau lourd et trivial—ponderous and trivial piece—is played by a wheezing ophicleide (an obsolete brass instrument) over a bass drum and pulsing strings while the pseudo-Balducci onstage mimes his approval. Next, pseudo-Balducci awards a prize to the singer of the bad piece in an elaborate metaphor that plays off the myth of the cuckoo and the nightingale, in which an incompetent judge favors the less sophisticated artist, which also lampoons Balducci's preference for Fieramosca over Cellini.

The crowd mocks the now-furious Balducci, as Teresa tries to find Cellini, who's disguised as a monk. Fieramosca, also disguised in the hope of making away with Teresa, enters. A swordfight breaks out between Cellini and Pompeo; Pompeo is killed: Ah, je suis mort!—Ah, I am dead! Bassoons gurgle as he dies, and Cellini cries out, Je suis perdu!—I'm done for! The composer continues to track everything that's going on, including revelers entering the piazza, with a phrase for flutes and strings from earlier in the scene that he shifts harmonically from major to minor as the action intensifies. The furious and swelling crowd captures Cellini, but distant cannon fire signals nightfall and the start of Lent. Candles are extinguished and Cellini, aided by Teresa, Ascanio, and other friends breaks away and escapes. A winding tune extracted from the *Messe solennelle* now takes over as the main theme of the racing chorus as some curse the cannon while the remaining members of Cellini's group bless it. Fieramosca in his monk's outfit is seized, as the chorus cries in real terror: La foule augmente, vous m'écrasez!—The crowd's growing, you're crushing me!

Act 2 opens with a somber orchestral introduction in which some themes from the previous scene are reiterated but shifted to minor keys and broken into shorter phrases. Teresa and Ascanio are found in Cellini's studio, where a plaster mold of his statue of Perseus stands in the background. Teresa is anxious about him, but Ascanio says his master is clever and tough. As they sing, a chorus of monks is heard passing from the street, chanting a prayer to the Virgin Mary. Ascanio and Teresa pray together: Sainte Vierge Marie, étoile du matin—Blessed Virgin Mary, morning star—their sweet tones cleverly contrasted verse for verse with the monks' chant, which is set in an archaic, hollow harmony suggesting the Middle Ages. The stage setting, with the heroine and her companion, as well as the musical phrasing of their prayer anticipates act 4 of Verdi's *Otello*.[69]

Cellini enters wearing a monk's habit, with Ascanio and Teresa equally relieved to see him. In a short, dashing narrative, Ma dague en main—Dagger in my hand—he describes his escape from the carnival: Ils n'ont pas pu me voir—They had lost track of me—and his return to the studio, where the monk's garb allowed him to fall in with a passing procession: Dans leurs rangs je me glisse à tout hasard—I slipped among them by chance. Trembling violins over twisting lines for the lower strings and barking brass interjections give the sense of a tale of danger, well told. Here, too, the composer wastes no opportunity, enriching Cellini's description of this day's dawn with a gorgeous phrase for flutes over padding pizzicato strings. Teresa now swears they will never be parted again, and Cellini says they must flee Rome at once. Ascanio asks about the statue, commissioned by the pope; Cellini's reply expresses anger and disgust: Au diable ma statue, et le Pape, et la loi!—To hell with my statue, the pope and the law!

Teresa and Cellini sing a duet that's shadowed with tension and anxiety as uncertainty and danger now color their view. Opening with a lilting orchestral phrase but in a melancholy minor key, Teresa take the first verse, Ah! Le ciel, cher époux—Beloved husband, heaven has spoken—to which Cellini replies fervently, Hâtons-nous de jouir de la paix—Let us hasten to enjoy that peace. From here they exchange lines rather than verses, as Cellini puts on armor should he need to fight his way out. They sing the opening verse together, in ever-mounting excitement; this leads to a quick-tempo closing passage, Quand des sommets de la montagne—When from the mountain's height—switching the analogy of the preceding passage to that of an eagle (here, Cellini) freeing its mate (Teresa) from a snare in which she is trapped. The composer sets it to agitated music featuring stiff and jerky rhythms for the singers and orchestra. Perhaps not the most appealing passage in the opera, it works reasonably well as the conclusion for the anxious love duet it follows but, between imagery and music, the scene feels overcrowded.

The closing dramatic sequence begins with a brief ensemble as Balducci and Fieramosca, who is now terrified of Cellini, enter his studio. Gloating that they've cornered him and calling him a murderer and seducer, they snipe at Cellini as he spits back his contempt; Balducci infuriatingly names Fieramosca as his son-in-law. The musical tone changes abruptly as the pope enters with his retinue and all drop to their knees. He is one of the best-drawn characters in *Benvenuto Cellini*; the libretto and Berlioz's music follow the shifting moods of a shrewd old politician and art patron with astonishing skill. To a slow and solemn brass-laden accompaniment, he begins benevolently, offering A tous péchés pleine indulgence—For all sins full indulgence. Balducci and Fieramosca ask for justice for their complaints, to which the pope blandly asks them to name the culprit. When Cellini is named, he responds with unconvincing shock, then asks Cellini, Tu feras donc toujours le diable, incorrigible garnement?—Will you always be a devil, incorrigible scamp?—a question that reveals his affection for the artist. Although he's guilty, Cellini tries to respond, but the pope cuts him off impatiently: Et ma statue, dis-moi, qu'est-elle devenue?—And my statue, tell me, what's become of it?—revealing what's really on his mind.

Cellini replies that it's not yet cast; the pope replies: Vraiment, je suis bien débonnaire—Truly, I am good-humored and patient—then says that someone else will have to cast it. Incensed, Cellini says that no one, Fût-il Michel-Ange, ma foi!—By God, were he Michelangelo himself—will cast it. The pope orders his guards to arrest Cellini, who jumps toward the cast with a hammer, melodramatically threatening to smash it: Non, avant que l'un d'eux me saisisse—Before a single one of them lays hands on me. The music of this scene reflects the rising tension in the room well, as scurrying string and barking brass underline the accelerating tempos and closer exchanges between the characters. With Cellini in control of the situation for the moment, the pope asks what will stop him from destroying the cast; Cellini replies, De mes fautes l'entier pardon—Full forgiveness for my sins—which the pope grants without hesitation; he then asks for Teresa's hand and more time to cast the statue. Muttering Quelle audace!—What impudence!—the pope and the others repeat Cellini's extortionate demands in shock.

The comic sextet (Cellini, Teresa, Ascanio, Balducci, Fieramosca, pope) is surely the high point of this tableau and one of the best scenes musically and dramatically in the opera, with Berlioz's treatment animating the shifting affects of the characters. Everyone has something different to say, with the pope exasperated and out of patience: Il sait pour l'art tout mon amour . . . mais avant peu j'aurai mon tour—He knows of my love of art . . . but soon my turn will come—which Balducci and Fieramosca echo. Teresa is petrified, while Ascanio is filled with admiration for his master: Oh! Noble hardiesse!—What superb audacity! Only Cellini seems oblivious of his own danger. When asked how long he needs to cast the statue, he replies that he can finish it today. The gurgling bassoons and clarinets that accompany the pope's opening phrase of the ensemble set an unmistakably comic tone, as does the stiff counterpoint in which the characters make their entries, which the composer breaks from and returns to with perfect ease as the sense of the text demands. As the pope agrees, he tells Cellini in a monologue of increasing intensity that he will return himself to see the completed statue; but if it's not done by then, Dès ce soir tu seras pendu. C'est, je le crois, bien entendu—You will hang tonight. Do I make myself clear? In the closing phrases, while Teresa and Ascanio comically chirp, pendu—hang—Cellini ironically thanks the pope. A short ensemble for the six characters that's clearly excessive in terms of text ends the scene. Begun by the pope, Ah! Maintenant de sa folle impudence—Now he will feel less proud—everyone has their say again, but now with too many words that at a quick tempo are inevitably garbled. But the music, loaded with the composer's best trademarks—rhythmic compressions, leaping lines, dazzling shifts in instrumental texture and harmony—moves with irresistible momentum.

The fourth tableau, set in the Colosseum, opens with the furnace for the casting hidden behind another curtain. Probably too long and event-filled for this point in the opera, it begins, after an atmospheric orchestral introduction, with two arias. The first is for the (relatively) innocent Ascanio where he expresses his anxiety in a lilting, semicomical number that also covers some exposition of plot. After admitting Mon âme est triste—My soul is sad, he sings some careless tra-la-las, then explains that their Enfant d'airan—Bronze child—is to receive its baptism of fire, with the Colosseum its church, and Le très Saint-Père—His Holiness—its godfather. But reviewing the day's events he grows nervous again, remembering that it might end with Cellini's hanging (Pendu! Pendu!) It's a well-judged bit of psychology on Berlioz's part as he finds ways to highlight Ascanio's wish to act carefree in spite of his fears.

Cellini's recitative and aria opens with a long, dark-hued meditation for strings that anticipates Faust's brooding Invocation to Nature from *La Damnation*. Isolated and now uneasy, Cellini sings of his struggle and of Rome, wishing he were elsewhere: Sur les monts les plus sauvages que ne suis-je un simple pasteur—On the wildest mountains why am I not a simple shepherd—which anticipates Herod's aria in *L'Enfance*. This beautiful and spacious setting where Cellini idealizes a life he cannot have, features much lovely commentary for the woodwinds and French horn that suggest the sounds of the flocks and fresh breezes away from the city. In the dreamy middle section, Cellini describes his chaumière—cottage—to a particularly rich accompaniment featuring intertwining lines for woodwinds. The closing part recapitulates the opening but with greater poignancy for the singer and to a more elaborate accompaniment.

A short but magical scene follows as a chorus of foundry-men from behind the curtain sings a delicate song, Bienhereux les matelots—Fortunate are sailors—that worries Cellini, who comments, Toujours avec cet air quelque malheur arrive—Some misfortune always comes when they sing it. (The song does end with L'onde est leur tombeau—The sea is their tomb.) But set in an interesting rhythm to offstage guitars and hand-cymbals, it presents a moment of strange, dreamlike beauty at this point of increasing dramatic tension. He and Ascanio try to encourage them by reminding them that they are sailors d'un fleuve de métaux—on a sea of metal. Fieramosca enters accompanied by two thugs. In dialogue, he tells Cellini that he's come t'envoyer en enfer—to send him to hell—but decides to wait while Cellini goes off to find his sword. All this business only impedes the drama at a crucial moment. Slightly less problematic is the vigorous if rather noisy chorus, Peuple ouvrier, que l'atelier vite se ferme!—Fellow workers, close the workshop at once!—as the fed-up foundry-men call a strike. With Cellini offstage, Teresa is left to plead with them to remain. There's more cliff-hanging business in dialogue as Cellini and Fieramosca argue. Seeing Cellini again, the workmen return to the foundry in a dusky but beautiful chorus punctuated by brighter-hued encouragement from Teresa and Ascanio.

The pope and his retinue arrive to a recapitulation of the solemn music that accompanied his entrance in the previous scene. He asks Cellini: Eh bien, démon, as-tu fini?—Well, you devil, have you finished? Cellini replies with his usual bravado but the pope and Balducci smell his defeat. Fieramosca, for some reason, has joined the foundry crew. To an impressive phrase for clarinets and trumpets over rushing strings he enters, calling, Du métal, du métal!—More metal! Cellini, then Balducci, are startled to see Fieramosca helping. He can only answer, Entre artistes ne doit-on pas s'entr'aider—We artists have to help each other. Cellini dashes back and forth between the foundry behind the curtain and the dignitaries onstage. But now he's nervous: they've really run out of metal to melt. Balducci mocks him that *un homme de génie*—a man of genius—must have a solution. The worldly Cellini cries out melodramatically but in a powerful and desperate recitative to God. Suddenly deciding to sacrifice his works that are also at the foundry, he has them brought inside for melting. In a short, exciting ensemble, the pope and others comment, *Son audace m'étonne!*—His nerve astounds me! There's an explosion; molten metal flows, signaling that the mold has overflowed; Cellini thinks he's failed, but the workers cheer: *Viva, viva, maître!*—Long live the master!—of his success. Fieramosca seems equally happy in Cellini's achievement as he is to share it; even Balducci claims he always knew that Cellini would succeed. And the pope—*Puisque Dieu lui-même a béni tes travaux et ta hardiesse*—Since God himself has blessed your labors and boldness—forgives Cellini and gives him Teresa's hand. *Benvenuto Cellini* ends with a final, compressed iteration of the metalworker's chorus from the second tableau, an ending that's satisfying enough, if "a bit conventional."[70]

Les Troyens, *Virgil* (... and Shakespeare)

His confidence buoyed by the successes of *L'Enfance du Christ* and the Te Deum, Berlioz started in 1856 and completed *Les Troyens*—The Trojans—two years later, a short gestation period for this long and complex work. *Les Troyens* has gradually become accepted as his masterwork, and the culmination of his life's work as a dramatic composer. Berlioz wrote the excellent libretto himself, based on books 1, 2, and 4 of Virgil's *Aeneid*. *Les Troyens* covers the fall of Troy in the first two of its five acts. The arrival of the Trojan refugees in Carthage, the love story of the Carthaginian Queen Dido (Didon in French) and the Trojan hero Aeneas (Énée), the departure of the Trojans for Italy and Dido's suicide in acts 3 through 5. It's a colossal music drama that takes four hours to perform, and although now generally spoken of with admiration and revived occasionally by major opera companies, *Les Troyens* likely remains the least-known great opera from an age that saw the creation of so many.

Setting classical epics and characters and incidents from them was common in early operas through the baroque era, with all the attendant inaction of set numbers and virtuoso singing. By the time Berlioz began work on *Les Troyens*, except for the showy vocalism insisted on by some singers (loathed and rejected by Berlioz for his own works), the aesthetic goals of opera had mostly changed, with a wide range of common characters expressing common passions having become standard. The dramatic character of *Troyens* is direct yet subtle, with its protagonists placed in the typical operatic dilemma of having to choose between love and responsibility. Their paradox is that Didon first expresses her sense of duty as a faithful widow and queen before yielding to love, while Énée falls in love readily then unhappily but without scruple leaves to fulfill his gods' demands. Warmhearted and wise yet passionate, Didon is the more appealing of the pair; Berlioz paints Énée as a war hero and man of destiny, whose rigidity stem both from his innate nature and upbringing as a military leader. The other major operatic work on the same subject is Purcell's *Dido and Aeneas*, a three-act, barely hour-long masterpiece from 1689, which differs as much as it might from Berlioz's vast work. The likelihood Berlioz knew Purcell's work is slim. But it's worth noting that both contain great final arias for Dido; and while you may agree that, in *Troyens*, "Aeneas is only a little less wooden than in Purcell . . ."[71] Berlioz treats him with a bit more depth and sympathy by giving him in passages in act 3, where he touchingly describes his upbringing and purpose to his own son, Ascanius (Ascagne in French).

The musical character of *Les Troyens* is admirably varied, but its prevailing tone is a Berlioizian nobility, reaching for grandeur in the composer's inimitable, sometimes quirky way. As leaders, Didon and Énée sing more freely in private, with public behavior phrased with an almost ceremonial regularity. When expressing their unease or pain alone or to intimates, as Didon does with her sister Anna in private confessions, the quality of their expression can be unmediated, even raw. Of course, Didon's two-part scene of desperation and resolve to die after the departure of Énée and the Trojans in act 5 (generally known by the opening line of the second part, Adieu, fière cité—Farewell, proud city) is agonized and one of the high points of the score and of the soprano repertory. But even Énée's act 5 recitative and aria expressing his misgivings about leaving Didon (Inutiles regrets—Futile regrets) makes his character genuine.

Didon is a soprano, Énée a tenor, and the Trojan princess Cassandre is supposed to be a mezzo-soprano though sopranos have sung the role successfully. The voices of other characters fall as expected, with older men sung by basses and so on. But it's hard to think of another music drama where vocal categories seem less relevant than *Les Troyens*. As mentioned, Berlioz despised vocal show for its own sake, and although there are a few high notes for the leads, these always grow directly from the flow of the musical and dramatic thought and pacing, and are never long-held. There's a consistent tone of noble gravity to the work that forbids the idea of vulgar display. Still, for variety of color and mood, Berlioz works in moments of lyrical beauty outside the high drama of the principal characters. Chief among these are the Carthaginian poet Iopas's hymn to Cérès, goddess of the harvest, in act 4, and the masthead song of the Trojan sailor Hylas that opens act 5. These set numbers stand on their own, but the composer finds opportunity for more, as we'll see.

Berlioz gives prominence to two thematic ideas, the Marche Troyenne—Trojan March—that accompanies the refugees, led by Énée, to Carthage, then away at the end of the opera; the other is the one word cry Italie, which obviously means Italy, where the gods want the Trojans to found a new empire. Italy is first mentioned in passing (if memorably) in act 2 by the ghost of the Trojan hero Hector, who appears to Énée, telling him that Troy has fallen and he must lead the Trojan survivors there. The word is sung again at the end of act 4, where the god Mercure (Mercury) appears, sternly uttering it three times. And act 5 contains many ever more alarming iterations by Trojans living and dead who remind Énée and his fellow refugees that they must leave Carthage. Anything but triumphant, the Trojan March is handled with remarkable subtlety over the course of the score, with each appearance different in tone and shading. The other melodic idea he repeats is the theme of the great love duet near the end of act 4, which Didon recalls desolately in her act 5 death song, Adieu, fière cité—Farewell, proud city. Thematic motifs don't recur repeatedly as in Wagner's works.

As with the vocal parts, Berlioz treats the orchestra more austerely than is his custom to suit the seriousness of his subject. There's nothing flashy or flamboyant to be heard, as in the *Symphonie fantastique* or *La Damnation de Faust*, with a few obvious exceptions. First are the dances and marches of acts 1, 3, and 4, where he allows himself more orchestral color to emphasize their exoticism. The spectral moments of acts 1 and 5 are also handled with greater freedom, with eerie instrumental effects that create fear and alarm. Finally, evoking a North African atmosphere, the big Chasse Royale et Orage—Royal Hunt and Storm—that opens act 4 is opulently scored, and is the orchestral high point of *Les Troyens*, as the composer intended.

Although Berlioz studied and adored Virgil from childhood, the composer also looked to Shakespeare, the other great literary idol of his formative years, for inspiration as well as for more practical modeling for this wildly ambitious theatrical work. We know of the composer's worship of Shakespeare not only from his words but also from the fact that the two major dramatic works covered in chapter 4 are based on Shakespeare. The dialogue transposed from *The Merchant of Venice* to the love duet in act 4 is the most obvious example, and is always cited. But there's more: the five-act form of *Les Troyens* belongs to French grand opera but is Shakespeare's as well. Perhaps most Shakespearean of all is the range of characters, from high to low, and everything in between. Ordinary men, represented by guards on duty who have settled easily into new lives in Carthage and a sailor dreaming of home dominate the beginning of act 5. Other imaginative stimuli from Shakespeare are "the far-flung topography of the action, in the elements of . . . the supernatural which are allowed their part . . ."[72]

The performance history of *Les Troyens* is not a happy one. Because it was deemed too difficult to mount by the Paris Opéra, the composer had to break the opera into two parts if he hoped to see any of it performed at all. These were acts 1 and 2, set in Troy and renamed *La Prise de Troie*—The Fall of Troy—with acts 3 through 5 dubbed *Les Troyens à Carthage*—The Trojans in Carthage—which was performed at a second-tier house, the Théâtre Lyrique, in 1863. Berlioz's music was well received, even though the staging was inadequate. It has been suggested that since the Trojan princess Cassandre and Queen Didon perform as separate, nonoverlapping heroines of these two parts there's some logic to the division.[73] But it's important to keep in mind that Berlioz was forced to cut the work up if he hoped to see any of it produced. Moreover, to hear the sweep and grandeur of *Les Troyens* is to understand the integrity of its five-act conception. The Berlioz renaissance of the mid-twentieth century restored the full opera to its original form. Still a work for a big, well-equipped house, the elaborate production demands of *Les Troyens* have kept stagings rare.

The sad background of its early performance history and its great length made *Les Troyens* easy to ignore. For close to a century, occasional excerpts, chiefly The Royal Hunt and Storm and the love duet, both from act 4, and Didon's farewell from act 5 were the most one might come across; an aria of Cassandre's (Malheureux roi—Ill-fated king) from act 1 has also had a bit of life apart from the complete opera. No less that Wagner's *Götterdämmerung* (which is also longer) or the five-act version of Verdi's *Don Carlos*, *Les Troyens* takes effort on the part of the audience or listener. It's an ambitious work with some flaws: chief among these are digressions from the storyline that contribute to a sense of drift, adding time to an opera that's already long and demanding. Examples can be found in acts 1, 3, and 4 where various processions and dances interrupt the dramatic progress. On the other hand, although not strictly relevant, the beautiful arias for Iopas (in act 4) and Hylas (act 5) at least offer commentary on the lead characters from other points of view. In any case, art conceived on the scale of operas like these are too big for perfection, their flaws entail no real shame on the composer's part. (*Götterdämmerung* has plenty!) The astute British musicologist and critic D. F. Tovey liked Berlioz but seemed to regard his affection as a guilty pleasure, often writing patronizingly about Berlioz's music. But this was the footnote Tovey appended to an essay he had written on *Roméo et Juliette*: "We must be careful! You never know where you are with Berlioz. Towards the end of March 1935 Dr. Erik Chisholm produced the whole of both parts of *Les Troyens* in Glasgow, and revealed it as one of the most gigantic and convincing masterpieces of music-drama."[74]

Set in a single, hour-long scene, act 1 opens the drama in Troy as Trojans celebrate, believing the Greeks have given up the war. Only Cassandre, the daughter of King Priam, who is gifted—or cursed—with prophecy, senses disaster in the wooden horse. That infamous object is brought into the city, as the Trojans celebrate their apparent victory with dances and wrestling. Énée rushes in with disturbing news: Laocoon, the high priest of Neptune, who had been suspicious of the horse, has been killed by snakes that swam out of the ocean. Cassandre sees that this is a bad omen, but the horse is brought into the city.

Berlioz gets right to business with a proto-cinematic fade-in, opening this epic tragedy of nations and their leaders with a joyful chorus for Trojans as they pour out of the city in which they have been trapped by the Greek armies for ten years. There's no big overture presenting themes like the Trojan March. Instead, the chorus opens with cries of joy before they can articulate their delight: Ah, quel bonheur de respirer l'air pur des champs—What delight to breathe the pure air of our fields! The music is set in a bounding, athletic 6/8 meter that captures their wonder and excitement at the regained freedom we know to be false. Some interesting harmonic clashes form part of the chorus's lines. In a second section, set in the rhythm of a country dance, there's further expression of joy and wonder. Perhaps most interesting from an instrumental standpoint is that this entire opening is set for winds, brass, and percussion only, with no strings to be heard.

The strings are introduced and with them a tragic tone with Cassandre's soliloquy, Les Grecs ont disparu—The Greeks have vanished. Set in two sections, the opening recitative is followed by a powerful aria against a majestic stalking rhythm for strings, as Cassandre questions these strange circumstances, invoking the ghost of the dead Trojan hero, her brother Hector; the ominous tone of muted horns joins the strings as she describes her vision. She's most troubled by her father, King Priam's participation in the misguided festivities, as expressed in her aria Malheureux roi—Ill-fated king. Set in a free three-part form with a contrasting middle section, the music builds to a climax on Malheureux peuple—Ill-fated people—where her line rises then moves on without flourish or fuss in a fine example of the composer's respect for Cassandre's tragic character, the somber nature of the drama and the integrity of the text. In the middle section, Cassandre bewails the fact that even her betrothed, Chorèbe, thinks she's mad: Chorèbe, hélas, croit ma raison perdue—Alas, Chorèbe thinks me out of my mind. This beautiful passage features ever shifting tonalities, as the composer mellows the instrumentation by adding clarinets. The closing part echoes the opening but alters its mood subtly as Cassandre tenderly reflects that she will never marry and that because Chorèbe, who's not a native of Troy, Il faut qu'il parte et quitte la Troiade—He must leave the Troiad. Berlioz seems to work as much meaning as imaginable into the closing bars, which are filled with menacing harmonic shifts in the lower brass.

Chorèbe enters; the two characters embark on a long, complex sequence that includes dialogue and aria. The distinctive, high-set, rhythmically agitated music that accompanies his entrance shows Berlioz's style at its purest. In a dialogue in recitative, Chorèbe tells Cassandre that everyone is now outside the walls and asking for her, but she replies that she's hiding because of Le trouble affreux dont mon âme est remplie—The terrible dread that fills my soul. In a short, lyrically masculine aria, called a *cavatine* (cavatina), he tries to calm her. Reviens à toi—Come back to yourself—Chorèbe's little aria, is richly orchestrated, painting this already appealing character as a kind and noble soul, as well. But Cassandre will not be soothed, as she embarks on a litany of the disasters she sees coming. The listing of bloodstained streets and shrieking, half-naked virgins, and Chorèbe's own death may evoke standard horrors. But Cassandre's music, mostly set for woodwinds and brass over a grinding figure for the lower strings to a steadily rising melody over a parallel harmonic underpinning, is chilling. Now accompanied by weeping woodwinds, Chorèbe resumes his consoling words, but Cassandre interrupts him continually, speaking to herself as much as him of the horrors to come.

Cassandre makes a final attempt to convince Chorèbe that he's wrong: Quitte-nous dès ce soir . . . pars ce soir, pars ce soir!—Leave us tonight, go tonight, go tonight! Of course, he will not be persuaded, hurling her own words back in an anguished accusation that she doesn't love him; all his emotions, love, disappointment, and his fundamental loyalty are captured and portrayed clearly. This leads into a duet for the two, set in a powerful, almost waltzlike beat. He finally reduces all his replies to her pleas and warnings by repeating his sturdy reply, Je ne te quitte pas—I will not leave you—and she finally cries out in despair: La mort jalouse prépare notre lit nuptial pour demain—Death makes ready our marriage bed for tomorrow. The composer ends this fierce duet with a potent, string-dominated instrumental postlude.

The tragedies of Cassandre and Chorèbe give way to less personal events and music as the Trojans march and solemnly thank Neptune, the city's patron god; this is followed by a short, relatively cheerful wrestling match that's effectively a ballet. The march and chorus Dieux protecteurs de la ville éternelle—Gods who watch our eternal city—is a substantial passage that depicts King Priam and the elite of Troy as they review the city's warriors, who pass in review. Notable for its lack of bombast, the five-minute march is marked by much overlapping canonic writing for the chorus, carefully calculated contrasts of dynamics and the continual harmonic shading typical of the composer. The percussion is almost continually at work but never intrusive. Although dominated by brass and percussion, the violins occasionally add high-set commentary when Neptune and the other gods are addressed: Régulateurs de l'univers, acceptez les présents de la reconnaissance—Rulers of the universe, accept our grateful offerings—as though depicting the upward gaze of the grateful Trojans. The vigorous ninety-second ballet (Combat de Ceste—Wrestler's Dance) is partly set in an unusual 5/8 meter, uncommon in Western music. It feels off-balance to our ears, and must have been used by Berlioz to capture the athletes' physical instability as they wrestle.

Private and public griefs are balanced of the next passage, titled "Pantomime," by the composer, and one of the remarkable moments in this score. Andromaque and Astyanax, the widow and young son of Hector, the dead Trojan hero, join the thanksgiving ceremonies outside the walls, but their grief is shown as deeply affecting to the entire populace. Moving at one steady tempo, and unified as well by a long, lamenting line for the clarinet, the scene opens with the bereaved pair entering and placing flowers at an altar; the chorus comments dolefully on the contrast between their sadness and the general sense of relief. Priam and his wife, Hécube (singing characters who perform silently here along with Andromaque and Astyanax who never sing, explaining the scene's title) greet them solemnly; the boy clings fearfully to his mother, whose émotion douloureuse . . . augmente—grief . . . increases—silently, of course. Cassandre passes by, warning that Andromaque should save her tears, because À de prochain malheurs tu dois bien des larmes amères—Disasters soon to come will make you weep long and bitterly—though Cassandre is essentially soliloquizing, as no one pays attention.

Although the astonishing solo for a weeping clarinet dominates the instrumental texture, other musical elements are worth listening for. Berlioz opens the scene in the mournful key of A minor, but paradoxically far more tragic in effect is the shift to A major (marked "Appassionato" in the score) normally a move that would create a sense of happy relief to the ears; here the tonal shift releases and amplifies the sense of grief. The instrumentation darkens considerably as Priam and Hécube bless Astyanax, with brushed cymbals adding a bit of nineteenth-century military color.

A six-minute scene in which Sinon, a Greek spy, is discovered and questioned about the wooden horse originally came next, but Berlioz cut it and it's usually skipped in recorded performances. The composer's decision to drop the scene from his final version made sense: "Berlioz saw that act I could proceed just as well from Andromache's pantomime to Aeneas's account of Laocoön and the serpents, so Sinon's scene was abandoned and later references to him rewritten."[75] Conductor and Berlioz specialist John Nelson omits it "because it ruins the dramatic entrance of Énée and was never orchestrated by Berlioz."[76] It's also skipped in Colin Davis's groundbreaking 1969 recording of *Troyens*. The scene can be heard on the 1994 recording with the Montreal Symphony led by Charles Dutoit.

In the next scene, a brief narrative in recitative, Énée dashes in, frantically describing how Laocoon, the high priest of Neptune, has been devoured by two serpents that emerged from the sea while he suspiciously probed at the wooden horse with a spear. Although brief, this is an effective bit of tone painting, as growling lower brass depict the twisting motion of the serpents. This leads directly into a huge ensemble, Châtiment effroyable!—Awful punishment!—for eight principals and chorus, expressing dismay at the fate of Laocoon. This slow-tempo exercise, Le sang s'est glacé dans mon coeur—The blood freezes in my heart—moves at a nearly frozen pace, depicting the Trojans' bewildered terror. Berlioz makes liberal use of stately dotted rhythms (short-*long*) as well as alternating dynamics, with some singers muttering while others shriek, to achieve something of the monumental feel of a baroque sacred work, like a Handel oratorio or one of Bach's Passions. The composer's harmonic language remains his own though; and the orchestra is unquestionably that of the mid-nineteenth century, with snarling trombones adding power to the climax.

In a brief dialogue in recitative and chorus, Énée and Priam agree that the gods are angry and to appease them the horse must be brought into the city at once. Everyone else agrees, as to a bustling accompaniment in a lilting rhythm, all but Cassandre exit. Over the Trojans' hopeful cries, she utters Malheur!—Doom!—twice in a minor-key wail that contrasts with their empty hopes. She remains onstage for her aria Non, je ne verrai pas la déplorable fête—No, I shall not watch their pitiful rejoicing. Short, intense, and potent, Cassandre speaks of her personal terror and dread of Troy's fate in a long, sinking melodic line set over churning strings and more lyrical lines for the woodwinds, particularly the clarinet. Toward the end, the accompaniment quiets as she sings in agony of Priam and Chorèbe, whose terrible fates she foresees. Cassandre's lament blends into the final number of act 1, in which the wooden horse is brought into the city.

This great closing scene, which includes the first appearance of the Marche Troyenne, is of great importance in the dramatic structure of the opera. Here, as in all its later appearances, the march carries the ambiguities of the linked myths of Troy and Rome. Berlioz never presents it in a fully triumphal garb, even at the end, when the glory of Rome is understood to be at the expense of Carthage and implicitly the other nations Rome will conquer; and Énée's flight from Carthage to found Rome brings personal ruin to Didon. More obviously ironic, and spelled out in the text is the folly of the Trojans who celebrate as they drag the wooden horse into the city.

Berlioz captures all of this, and more. The fanfare-laden march is heard first from offstage brass, with the chorus hailing its arrival and praying to Minerva, the Latin incarnation of Athena, to protect them: Belle Pallas, protège-nous—Fair Pallas [a Greek name for Minerva; both names are used], protect us. Appalled, Cassandre listens then watches as the crowd nears and the horse appears: L'énorme machine roulante s'avance! . . . La voici!—The great engine rolls onward—there it is! The music builds in intensity, with the march, the hymning of the chorus, and Cassandre's desperate comments all together and always sharply contrasted. The harps enter, always the sign with Berlioz of an approaching musical climax. Powerful, syncopated notes for the full orchestra add to the tension. Some near the horse hear from inside a startling bruit d'armes—clang of arms—as Cassandre cries out to Jupiter and hopes for a moment that sanity may return and that the horse will be searched. But the sound is misinterpreted as a good omen, as the progress of the horse continues. It's too late as, Cassandre tells herself: Soeur d'Hector, va mourir sous les débris de Troie!—Sister of Hector, go, die beneath the ruins of Troy! The composer closes the scene that began in ambiguous triumph with cadences that predict disaster.

The fall of Troy takes place in act 2, which is divided into two scenes. In the first, Énée is visited by the ghost of Hector, who warns him that the city has fallen and he must refound it in Italy. A wounded Chorèbe passes, telling Énée that the citadel is still holding out. In the second scene, set in the citadel, the Trojan women, led by Cassandre, swear to die rather than endure rape and enslavement at the hands of the Greeks. As the Greeks enter, the women carry out their oath.

Sounds of battle are heard in the distance as Énée sleeps. The composer opens the act with substantial introduction while several other characters crossing the stage, some in pantomime. The troubled, proto-cinematic accompaniment features trembling violins over a dragging figure for the lower woodwinds and strings, interspersed with trumpet calls offstage. The music brightens a bit as Ascagne, Énée's son, enters, alarmed at the sounds from afar. The ghost of Hector, bloodstained and grimy as at his death, enters to snarls from muted French horns and stealthy plucked strings. A loud crash wakes Énée who, troubled by the light and sounds, asks his city in a recitative: Ô lumière de Troie . . . quel nuage semble voiler tes yeux sereins?—Oh, light of Troy . . . what veil seems to cloud your noble eyes? He's told grimly by Hector's ghost, who addresses him as fils de Vénus—son of Venus—that Troy has fallen, though they fought together Pour sauver la patrie, sans l'arrêt du destin—To save our country, but for the decree of fate. Hector tells him: Va, cherche l'Italie, où pour ton peuple renaissant . . . tu dois fonder un empire puissant, dans l'avenir, dominateur du monde—Go, seek Italy where for your people reborn . . . you are to found a mighty empire, destined to rule the world. Berlioz sets this prophecy, and Hector's entire warning, to the darkest music in the score, concluding with a brief postlude in the same pitch-black orchestration and tone of mystery.

The near-motionlessness of the exchange with Hector's ghost contrasts with the furious calls to arms and busy activity of the next passage, in which Trojans warriors make one last, futile attempt to save the city. The Trojan warrior Panthus enters, wounded, carrying some of the city's sacred items; he informs Énée, C'est notre jour fatal! Priam n'est plus!—Out last day has come! Priam is no more!—then describes the cunning deceit of the Greek horse. Chorèbe enters, telling Grand Énée—Great Aeneas—that the citadel is still holding out. Placing Ascagne in the care of some soldiers and crying: Le salut des vaincus est de n'en plus attendre—One safety the vanquished have: to hope for none—Énée leads his men into battle.

The second scene, set in the palace of Priam, is shrewdly structured, opening quietly then rising tidally as the action intensifies. In the opening part, a chorus of Trojan women echoed by the high woodwinds prays to the goddess Cybele to intercede and save them and their city. Their lilting incantation, Puissant Cybèle—Mighty Cybele—has a strange, wailing, proto-orientalist sound, with and open harmonic shading that floats away from the cadences—the harmonic landings—Western ears anticipate and expect. Reminiscent of moments in *L'Enfance du Christ*, it's quite beautiful. Intimations of trouble can be sensed in rumbling from the lower strings and later, brass fanfares that remind us that the battle is closing in.

Cassandre enters, les cheveux épars—her hair disheveled—as noted in her stage direction. She brings good news: following three brave attempts to save the citadel, Énée and his troop have escaped with sacred relics of Troy to go to Italy, where une nouvelle Troie—a new, more beautiful and powerful city—will rise. This receives a proud-marchlike setting, but the musical background droops again as she tells the women that Chorèbe is dead. French horns signal the opening of Cassandre's mighty self-immolation, as she muses that this is la dernière fois—the last time—at the altar and that cet instant termine mon inutile vie—this moment ends my fruitless life. To an intensifying accompaniment of pulsing triplets for the woodwinds, the chorus praises her: Ô digne soeur d'Hector—Worthy to be Hector's sister—recalling bitterly that the city could have been saved even yesterday if her warning had been heeded. As the women quail, Cassandre rouses their patriotic pride, drawing her own dagger and showing the rest theirs to running figures in tightening phrases for the strings. She asks: Le jour ne vous trouvera pas par les Grecs profanées?—The morning will not find you defiled by the Greeks?

Most swear rapturously in a hymn, in which the sound of harps, depicting lyres the women play onstage, dominates and set to a sweeping dance rhythm. But a few, fearing death, hold back. Cassandre and the others mock them ferociously: Honte sur vous! Sortez! Vous n'êtes pas Troyennes!—Shame upon you! Get out! You are not Trojan women!—and the frightened women leave. The rest resume their mighty dance with death, picking up their lyres, the harps again dominating the orchestra, as Greek soldiers enter. In chorus, the soldiers threaten the women and cry out for the treasure, which as we know has departed with Énée. Cassandre spits her reply: Nous méprisons votre lâche menace . . . vous n'étancherez pas, brigands, votre soif d'or!—We scorn your cowardly threats . . . You will not quench your thirst for gold, thieves! Joining the ensemble, a Greek captain comments in awe at Cassandre: De ce noble transport j'admire malgré moi la sublime ironie . . . quelle est belle ainsi chantant la mort, Bacchante à l'oeil d'azur s'enivrant d'harmonie!—Against my will I'm struck by the sublime irony of their magnificent fervor . . . how beautiful she [Cassandre] looks as she sings of death, a blue-eyed Bacchante drunk with her own music!

Cassandre stabs herself, then passes the dagger to her sister Polyxène, who does the same. The rest of the women stab themselves or jump off the parapet; more Greeks enter, crying out in rage that the treasure is gone. With their dying breaths, the Trojan women apostrophize Énée, now well on his way: Sauve leur fils, Énée, Italie! Italie!—Save their sons, Aeneas! Italy! Italy!

An interesting aspect to this stirring scene is that although the action and consequently the music is episodic, its overall sense is one of torrential forward motion. Berlioz changes the pace and tone of the music repeatedly to reflect the words and stage action; but the crazed rapture of the Trojan women's anthem, carried on the sound of harps, sweeps everything in its path.

Set in Carthage, act 3 opens with ceremonies in which Didon greets her subjects, who hail her. She honors builders, sailors, and farmers for their contributions to the city's prosperity. Alone, her sister Anna predicts that Didon (a widow) will love again. The refugees from Troy, led by a disguised Énée, arrive and are admitted to the court. The introduction of the Trojans is interrupted by news of an attack on the city. Énée leads the combined forces of Carthage and the Trojans into battle against the invader.

Over a bounding rhythmic accompaniment, the citizens of Carthage, (which is only seven years old at this point) sing happily of its rapid growth and of the beauty of the day: De Carthage les cieux semblent bénir la fête—The heavens seem to bless Carthage on this festive day. As Didon and her court enter, the citizens launch into their anachronistic national anthem, Gloire à Didon, notre reine chérie—Glory to Dido, our beloved queen—serious in tone and long-winded, a specimen of nineteenth-century musical nationalism dropped into an ancient setting. If heavy, it's also unambiguously proud and happy, in contrast with the Trojans' March. (As we'll see, Berlioz revisits the anthem at the end of the scene with a musically richer iteration.) From her throne, Didon narrates the brief history of Carthage: Nous avons vu finir sept ans à peine depuis la jour—Barely seven years have passed since the day—going on to relate her husband's murder and their flight from Tyre (on the eastern Mediterranean coast) to North Africa. Refugees themselves, the founders of Carthage have flourished in their new home; Didon thanks them again: Chers Tyriens, tant de nobles travaux ont enivré mon coeur d'un orgeuil légitime—Dear Tyrians, your noble and unstinting work has gladdened my heard with justifiable pride. She says that now she's sure they will be as brave in war as in peace, to which the crowd cheers in agreement. She also relates how she has turned down the marriage proposal of le farouche Iarbas—sullen Iarbas (king of Numidia): Son insolence est vaine—Whose insolence is in vain; the crowd cheers its endorsement of her decision.

Berlioz's accompaniment of course shifts with the tone of the text, but the composer maintains throughout a regal and even somewhat high-strung tone. He accomplishes this by liberally deploying an old-fashioned dotted rhythm (short-*long* . . .) that has denoted majesty in music since at least the baroque era. He also uses his own distinctive nervous touch in the commentary of strings and high woodwinds that are one of his clearest stylistic signatures. (These come in immediately after "Chers Tyriens" and continue through Didon's aria.) As this exposition of background is fairly long, Berlioz shifts the rhythmic accompaniment to steady pulsation that's calmer than the noble dotted rhythm, which, however, he brings back toward the end, as the chorus rejoins in praise.

Les Troyens, Virgil (. . . and Shakespeare) 129

Didon invites the builders, sailors, and farm laborers to present themselves as they approach in a brief, three-part mimed interlude that's quirky like most of the composer's choreographed entr'actes, but also of great charm. The builders entrance is curious musically for having a distinct marchlike feel, despite being in 3/4 time, which is more commonly a dance beat. (Schumann ends his 1834 piano masterwork *Carnaval* with a brilliant 3/4-time march.) Onstage, Didon presents their chief with a measuring square made of silver and an ax. The sailors' march is also rhythmically peculiar, with angular entrances for the low strings and cheerful punctuation for the piccolos; their leader receives a rudder and an oar. The farm laborers, led by un viellard robutse—a robust old man—join the other groups. Their music, set in a more straightforward rhythm, is, however, accompanied by an exotic oboe solo that descends to the lower woodwinds, set against trilling violins. There are also more shifts from major to minor and back than with the first two groups. Didon presents the "viellard" with a golden sickle while in an aside offering heartfelt thanks to Cérès—Ceres, the goddess of the harvest, for her beneficence.

The citizens sing the national anthem once more as they march out in procession before Didon and her sister Anna. This second iteration works better than the first, thanks to enriched contrapuntal activity and greater rhythmic variety. Its antiphonal style, where two choruses respond to one another, is a passage of great breadth reminiscent of Handel's big choral movements with a stately walking bass line that is a stylistic trademark of the baroque master.

The dialogue between the sisters Didon and Anna that follows is of great delicacy, contrasting with the big-boned chorus it follows. Opening with a sequence of nervous, high-set sighs for the violins and woodwinds, Didon comments on how well things are going: Les chants joyeux, l'aspect de cette noble fête ont fait rentrer la paix en mon coeur agité—These happy hymns, the sight of this splendid festival, have brought peace back to my troubled heart. With the insight of a close sibling, Anna senses that Didon needs to share what's troubling her: Quelle crainte avait pu vous troubler un instant?—What fears can have disturbed you for an instant? A strange sadness—Une étrange tristesse—sometime oppresses her. Grasping Didon's real feelings, Anna smiles and gets right to the point: Vous aimerez, ma soeur—You will love again, my sister. Accompanies by sighing flutes, Didon protests that it's not possible, that she, La veuve fidèle doit éteindre son âme et detester l'amour—A faithful widow must subdue her soul and abhor love. Anna, now more playfully, interrupts Didon's complaint with repetitions of her promise that she will love again. To herself, Didon agrees, while Anna notes her sister's weakening will.

Introduced by flutes and French horns over trembling stings, the duet moves to Didon's richly expressive, proto-Straussian confession, Sa voix fait naître dans mon sein la dangereuse ivresse—Her words arouse in my breast a dangerous delight—as this great woman who takes her responsibilities very seriously admits that something is missing from her life. Anna sings separately but in agreement as the royal sisters consider Didon's situation from their own perspectives in a meltingly beautiful duet. Didon apostrophizes Sichée—Sychaeus—her late husband: Pardonne à cet instant d'involontaire erreur—Forgive this moment of unwilling delusion—while Anna asks Didon to forgive her if—Ma voix excite dans ton coeur ce trouble qui l'étonne—My words excite in your heart the unease that perturbs it.

Iopas, Didon's court poet, enters, bringing news of refugees, just landed after enduring a dangerous storm at sea, who request an audience. The queen replies, La porte du palais n'est jamais défendue à de tels suppliants—The doors of my palace are never closed to suppliants like these. She then sings a brief but touching aria, Errante sur les mers—A wanderer on the seas—in which she recalls the perils of her flight from Tyre. Her monologue is notable for the way certain phrases of the text, particularly Qui connut la souffrance ne pourrait voir en vain souffrir—One who has known suffering cannot look on when others suffer—are emphasized by repetition and a rising sigh for the flutes and violins. Didon's warmth and kindness are amplified by this two-minute character study.

The Trojan March with a new coloring is heard as the Trojans enter, Énée disguised as a sailor for the sake of the dramatic revelation of his identity that soon follows. The composer's heading for this iteration is Marche Troyenne dans la mode triste—Trojan March in the sad mode—and indeed, now the fanfares are set in minor keys with flashes of major tonalities that emphasize the movement's gloom. The march is instrumental except for one significant line for Didon, set over trembling strings: J'éprouve un soudaine et vive impatience de les voir, et je crains en secret leur présence—I feel a sudden, sharp impatience to see them, yet in my heart I fear their coming—which speaks to her sense of fate. Subdued but beautiful, this exquisitely orchestrated passage starts with the brass, then moves to woodwinds accompanied by strings in a somber phrase, dominated rhythmically by the suave motion of triplets. The instrumentation then shifts to violas and cellos, and the final, fragmented thematic statement is again given to the brass. Any doubt about the influence of Berlioz on Mahler disappears when one hears this passage, so predictive of the Austrian master's style in both symphonic movements (it could fit easily into the Symphony No. 7) and his songs.

To solemn chords, Ascagne, (Énée's son, a boy's role performed by a woman) steps forward as the Trojan spokesman. He offers Didon the treasures with which the Trojans escaped: d'Hécube la couronne, et ce voile léger d'Hélène où l'or rayonne—[Queen] Hecuba's crown, and this light veil, glistening with gold, Helen's. He reveals that they are Trojans, and to a triumphant fanfare—Notre chef est Énée—Our chief is Aeneas. Didon quietly replies, Étrange destinée—Strange fate. Panthée, one of the Trojan leaders, explains further that they seek Italy on the order of the gods. Didon proudly welcomes them to Carthage.

To trademarked nineteenth-century music depicting agitation, Narbal, one of Didon's ministers, enters with the bad news that Iarbas (the Numidian king whose proposal of marriage the queen tuned down), avec d'innombrables soldats—with hordes of soldiers—is attacking Carthage. Dressed magnificently and wearing a breastplate, Énée drops the sailors's disguise, identifying himself to Didon in a proud recitative, Reine, je suis Énée—Queen, I am Aeneas. He suggests that the Trojans should fight alongside the Carthaginians, and Didon immediately accepts, also falling in love with him on the spot, as she comments to Anna, Qu'il est fier, ce fils de la déese, et qu'on voit sur son front de grâce et de noblesse!—How superb he is, this son of the goddess, what grace and nobility are on his brow! In accelerating movement, the Trojans and Tyrians sing jointly that the Numidian had better tremble;

in another tremendous pronouncement, Énée proclaims to the Trojans L'enterprise nouvelle où la gloire les appelle—The new adventure that glory calls them to.

Énée leaves Ascagne in the care of Didon, who warmly replies that she will look after him de mon amour de mère—with a mother's love—strengthening her attraction and their connection. Énée then takes Ascagne aside in a tender but slightly stiff moment in which the father tells his son that others will have to teach him the art of happiness, because he can only instruct him in the ways of war and honor. Berlioz frames Énée's emotional limitations in sturdy, almost rigid phrasing for singer and orchestra, though commentary from a solo clarinet contributes a softer tone. To symbolize the code he will someday pass to Ascagne, Énée places his armor on the boy while singing. Carthaginians enter, noisily asking for arms to fight for their city, and a big, rackety chorus in which Trojans and Carthaginians agree follows: Volons à la victoire ensemble!—We'll sweep to victory side by side!

Big operatic choruses for crowds like these have a generic noisiness that even Berlioz cannot steer clear of completely; but even here he maintains his quirks of style, including a fine wind-down for the orchestra. And the private moments for principals and even secondary characters are set apart and quite convincing.

Set in two scenes, act 4 is framed by two enormous numbers, the mostly orchestral hunt and storm at its start and the great duet for Didon and Énée at the end. The opening scene depicts a sultry morning, as Didon and Énée, out hunting, become separated from their entourage. As a huge storm approaches they enter a cave for shelter, where they consummate their love. While some nymphs and satyrs celebrate, others cry out the one-word warning "Italy!" In scene 2, set in Didon's palace, Anna suggests to Didon's counsellor Narbal that Énée would make a fine husband; but Narbal warns that Italy is Énée's destiny. Didon and Énée watch a sequence of dances, and listen to a song by her court poet. The couple discuss the fall of Troy and the postfall histories of the surviving Trojans. The act ends with a love duet between the pair. At the very end, Mercure (Mercury) appears, pointing seaward and singing one word: Italie!

Les Troyens, Virgil (. . . and Shakespeare)

In the early days of the Berlioz renaissance, before the stature of *Les Troyens* was fully recognized, the Chasse royale et Orage—Royal hunt and storm—that opens act 4 was occasionally performed as an extract (or as Wagner might have called it, a "bleeding chunk") on its own. Charles Munch, the music director of the Boston Symphony Orchestra from 1949 to 1962 and one of the great performer-advocates for the composer, recorded the Hunt and Storm in 1961, without the chorus that adds so much to the music's effect. (This must have been an economy by RCA, the company that recorded the BSO at the time rather than Munch's idea.) Even without the strange and potent choral presence, it's a beautiful performance of this great passage that must have led some listeners to wonder about the rest of the opera.

While perhaps less familiar, Berlioz's stands high among orchestrally depicted storms, with other examples by Beethoven in the Symphony No. 6; Rossini in the overture to *Guillaume Tell*; Wagner in the opening scene of *Die Walküre*; and tremendous specimens by Verdi from *Rigoletto* and *Otello*. The closing movement of Debussy's symphonic poem *La Mer* depicts an oceanic tempest. Every example just cited uses music to describe in tones the sound and sense of a storm. Like the operatic scenes of Wagner and Verdi, the passage that opens act 4 of *Les Troyens* also carries elements of myth and legend as well as a dramatic narrative.

Set in "an African forest in the morning" and described by the composer in the score as a "Pantomime" (the second of two), the scene opens with a detailed description of the stage setting and an elaborate scenario that includes:

> Two naiads [water-nymphs] appear . . . Hunting calls resound far off in the depths of the forest. The frightened naiads hide in the reeds. Tyrian huntsmen pass, with dogs on leashes. Young Ascanius gallops across the stage on horseback. The sky darkens; it begins to rain. The storm grows. It becomes a tempest with sheets of rain, hail, lightning and thunder. Repeated hunting calls are heard amid the tumult . . . Dido and Aeneas appear, she dressed as Diana the huntress, bow in hand . . . he in semi-military dress. Both are on foot as they enter the cave. Immediately the nymphs of the forest appear with disheveled hair . . . [the nymphs] run back and forth, shouting and gesticulating wildly. In the midst of their yells, one

word can from time to time be heard: "Italy." The stream swells and becomes a torrent. Several other waterfalls form at different points . . . Satyrs and sylvans [spirits of the woods], with fauns, perform grotesque dances in the darkness. A tree is struck by lightning, shatters and catches fire . . . The satyrs, fauns and sylvans pick up the flaming branches and dance with them in their hands, then disappear with the nymphs into the depths of the forest. The storm passes. The clouds lift.[77]

It should be obvious from this extract, which only represents about three-quarters of Berlioz's description of the setting and action, that his imagination and dramatic ambitions are at high tide. The proto-cinematic visuals for this scene look back to the kind of loose ideas he had for *Faust* and ahead to what would later become possible in film and much later as special effects onstage in the opera house. And it's not just a storm he's composing, but a storm with a hunting scene right through the middle. The plot is here advanced by nature, a force far greater than the human protagonists, although they are pushed by love and desire, senses everyone knows and grasps. And all are subject to the commentary of the minor classical divinities onstage, from the shy naiads to the satyrs who incarnate lust.

The approach of a storm from a distance can satisfy and thrill. It's a favorite pictorial device of composers, and the one Berlioz employs here. Opening at a moderate volume and slow tempo, the scene opens with a broad theme for flutes and violins that will recur throughout and return at the end as calm returns after the storm. Woodwinds, including trills for the flutes and later other instruments, dominate this opening passage. Quick, nervous chords for the piccolos and flutes accompany the naiads' entrance, while soft rumbling from the timpani depicts distant thunder. A spacious and admirably asymmetrical melody enters in the flutes, accompanied by plucked strings; trills for piccolos round out this opening part.

The second part, depicting the passage of the hunters, moves at a quicker pace and different rhythm, the bounding 6/8 that told listeners of the eighteenth, nineteenth, and twentieth centuries that hunting was the musical or as here, musical-dramatic topic. Heard from a hazy distance, the hunting call is specified for a brass instrument called the sax-

Les Troyens, Virgil (. . . and Shakespeare)

horn, invented by Adolphe Sax, also designer of the much better-known saxophone.[78] The call, so distant as to seem tranquil, contains what has been described as a "blue note,"[79] the flattened tone that's characteristic of American Delta blues, and so striking as part of Berlioz's harmonic shading here. What might be the scrambling of terrified prey in faster notes and pounding horses' hooves are now heard as several hunters appear onstage.

That 6/8 rhythm can serve as a gentle dance, but here it pounds vigorously, if not quite violently, as the hunters cross the scene. A long theme for trombones signals the approach of the storm, as the saxhorn hunting theme now appears with more minor key inflections, suggesting the hunters' disarray in the shrieking gusts. The composer now cuts loose the full violence he's been keeping in check, as screaming woodwinds, roaring brass, pounding timpani, and scurrying strings depict the storm at its height, with the fragmented hunting theme worked in but subordinated to the storm. As soon as Didon and Énée discover and enter the cave where they will shelter in a tableau that's clearly erotic, as the drenched minor divinities burst out in a wordless cry of triumph, followed by "Italie!" Piccolos and timpani capture the effect of lightning and thunder, as surprising changes of tonality and rhythmic compressions suggest the storm's final spasms. A falling chromatic scale tells us that the scene is now completely hidden by clouds as the spacious melody from the opening returns. Finally, the sound of the hunter's horn returns again against quieting and slowing background patterns, ending in near-stillness.

Scene 2 opens with a dialogue in recitative between Anna and Narbal in which the story is advanced in narrative form. Anna asks Narbal why he's uneasy, now that Iarbas has been defeated; her question trailed by a playful, waltzlike figure for strings. Narbal agrees but says that Didon has begun to neglect her royal duties, and that En chasse, en festins, elle passe sa vie—She spends her time hunting and feasting. As a result, building has slowed and—les ateliers déserts—workshops stand empty. That the Trojans remain in Carthage worries him above all. To this Anna replies lightly, to a longer iteration of the playful waltz, that Didon and Énée are in love. Narbal is shocked by this news even though it seems like something everyone around them would know. Anna thinks Énée would make a splendid king, but Narbal reminds her over trembling strings that Le destin impérieux appelle Énée en Italie—Inexorable fate calls Énée to Italy. She replies that love, Le plus grand des dieux—The greatest of the gods—must also be obeyed; Anna's playful waltz leads to a duet between the two.

Set in three parts, the duet first expresses Narbal's justified fears, then Anna's light-hearted but erroneous assumption that everything will be fine. Berlioz then combines the two ideas, wholly opposite musically as in attitude, in a closing passage. There are a few surprises here from a musical standpoint, as the wise bass Narbal worries at a slow tempo, his orchestral accompaniment set for the low-pitched instruments across the orchestra but dominated by muttering heavy brass. Anna's light-hearted reply is set to a full version of the playful waltz heard in embryo in the previous dialogue, set to high woodwinds and pizzicato strings. Her last line is a good one: Bientôt ils vont s'unir. Telle est la menace du sombre avenir—Soon they'll be united: that's the disaster your dark future has in store. The two wildly different ideas are then joined in a remarkable duet in which both musical postures are maintained in one of those slightly self-conscious displays of skill at combination that Berlioz liked to perform. At the end, Anna's playfulness has the last word.

To an exquisitely scored version of the Carthaginian anthem, Didon, Énée, and their entourages enter. Far more delicate than the thunderous first version in act 3, this features the tune played by high woodwinds decorated by a dreamy string accompaniment. A substantial three-part ballet follows. First, Egyptian dancing girls perform in two contrasting sections. The first part is in graceful slow-motion accompanied by woodwinds and strings; in the second, punchier section, the brass join the ensemble. A vigorous Dance of the Slaves, featuring swoops by the piccolos and trills for the flutes follows. Filled with melodic and rhythmic and shifts, this passage is set in three broad sub-sections, the outer two driven seemingly by nervous impulses and the short middle part set to a beautiful chorographic melody. Last and shortest of the ballets is the Dance of the Nubian Slaves. In this moment of calculated exoticism, a small chorus sings in a made-up language, like the demons near the end of *Faust*, while flutes, violins, and a tambourine dominate the accompaniment. Unlike the previous dances, this moves at a steady pulse, but with strong accents that vary its rhythm. Although well executed and charming, these dances halt the action for a good ten minutes.

A restless Didon tells Anna to end the dances. She then asks her court poet Iopas to sing his Poème des champs—Poem of the fields. Accompanied onstage by a "Theban harpist," Iopas sings this beautiful and vocally difficult five-verse ode to Cérès, goddess of the harvest, whom Didon thanked particularly for her beneficence in act 3. Berlioz pays great attention to the accompaniments, which remain delicate but complex through each verse, varying them with great care. A harp in the orchestra which plays throughout, backed by woodwinds and strings set the rhythm in a lilting 6/8, as Iopas opens his song, Ô blonde Cérès—O Golden Ceres—first thanking her for the fraîche verdure—fresh young crops—that adorn the fields of Carthage. An oboe in contrary motion comments sweetly on Iopas's vocal line. In the second verse, the poet takes a more fervent tone as he sings of Du vieux labourer, du jeune pasteur—The old farm-worker, the young shepherd—who thank Cérès for her generosity. Verse 3 repeats the opening, but with the singer's and orchestral parts extended and varied. The basic melody of the first verse gets broken into shorter notes that add intensity but are never showy, though the singer (a tenor) has a couple of high ones to hit and he's echoed rapturously by the woodwinds. Berlioz picks up the tempo a bit to illustrate the animation contained in the fourth verse, describing Le timide oiseau, le folâtre agneau, des vents de la plaine—The timid bird, the frisky lamb, the soft breezes—signs of nature that also show Cérès's blessings. Like the previous verse this displays an ardent quality, with the singer's line high-set and passionately expressive. In the fifth and closing verse, the opening and third are repeated with one variation: the goddess is addressed as Féconde Cérès—Fruitful Ceres—over a steadily moving accompaniment, as at the end Iopas must hit two high notes; neither is long-held and both serve to emphasize the ecstasy of the text-setting. As you can tell, Ô blonde Cérès is one of the lyrical gems in this mighty score.

In the following two numbers, the first a dialogue in recitative followed by a quintet clarify Didon's restlessness and its cause, her love and desire for Énée. Her feelings of guilt and resistance to that desire collapse. Subtle stage action also moves the plot along. As Énée sits at

Didon's feet, she asks him to finish the story of Troy and of the fate of the Trojan nobility. Didon is shocked to hear that Andromaque (Hector's widow, whom we saw in the act 1 pantomime) has given in to the pleas of Pyrrhus, one of the Greek leaders, and married the man who killed her father. To this news she indignantly cries, Ô pudeur!—For shame!—then asks herself why she has stayed faithful to the memory or her husband when Tout conspire à vaincre mes remords et mon coeur est absous—Everything conspires to overcome my remorse, and my heart is absolved.

The final three numbers of act 4—the quintet, the septet, and the duet—make up an enormous structural unit that moves toward tranquility, at least until Mercury's proclamation at the very end. In the quintet that follows, Didon and Énée sing with their typical regal dignity, while Anna, Iopas, and Narbal playfully comment on what the two leads are doing. In the meantime, Ascagne (dressed as Cupid) and Didon perform a little pantomime in which he removes her late husband's ring from her finger. While repeating her justification, (Tout conspire . . .), she takes back the ring but leaves it on the couch on which she's sitting, symbolizing that she has moved on and permitted herself to love Énée. Didon and Énée sing initially over a pulsing accompaniment, while bassoons and lower strings play an anxious figure in sixteenth-notes below which gradually retreats as Didon's qualms fade. This is music that shows how seriously Didon takes her responsibilities and how hard it is for her to let them go. As the other three comment (Voyez, Narbal, la main légère de cet enfant, semblable à Cupidon . . .—Narbal, see how the light-fingered boy, like Cupid . . .) Berlioz lightens the accompaniment to skittering violins and rapidly pulsing woodwinds. But before the end, the composer returns all five to the serious tone in which he opened this gorgeous ensemble.

Ascagne and Narbal make up the last two soloists in the septet in which the chorus also joins. This intense and dark-hued ensemble, in which all share the same text, Tout n'est que paix et charme autour de nous—Peace and enchantment surround us—is a bit of tone painting that depicts the clear night that has fallen. The melody is a long, winding, and peaceful, set in a persistent three-note pattern which all but Didon keep to; she decorates it gently but noticeably in this mostly homophonic context. Powerful minor-key inflections depict the darkness as the steady pulsing of woodwinds suggest the gentle chirping of insects. Berlioz employs a pedal point, meaning a single tone that carries throughout the number, as a harmonic stabilizer. All the composer's technical wizardry is in service of a conception of hypnotic beauty.

The sky clears; the moon rises, and as the other characters gradually leave the stage Didon and Énée begin their great duet, Nuit d'ivresse et d'extase infinie—Night of boundless ecstasy and rapture. For all its amorous bliss, Berlioz structures the passage carefully, alternating verses in which the human lovers sing together with exchanges that refer to mythological couples. This, the composer adapted from the dialogue for Lorenzo and Jessica that opens act 5 of Shakespeare's *The Merchant of Venice*, rather than from Virgil.[80] Each of these exchanges is opened with the words: Par une telle nuit—On such a night—with the references to lovers of legend following. Although the lovers have left the stage by the time Mercure (Mercury) appears, the scene ends with his spectral appearance, as he bangs on Énée's shield while uttering the command "Italie," shattering the tender mood of the duet.

Didon and Énée sing three sets of paired verses, with an extra verse for Énée in the middle. In the first, their sweetly harmonized, tender melody is set to accompaniment for muted strings to a gentle rowing rhythm in which three-note patterns dominate. The first note of three is typically accented, creating a gentle but persistent rhythmic tug. A clarinet introduces the first of the exchanges, as Didon sings about Énée's parents, Anchises and the goddess Venus, over a gently syncopated accompaniment for woodwinds; Énée's ardent reply refers to the Trojan lovers, Hector's brother Troilus and la belle Cressida—the lovely Cressida. The refrain (Nuit d'extase . . .) is repeated, decorated by the singers, Didon's in even notes and Énée's in a more elaborate rhythm but both quite chastely. To excited but still delicate trills and runs for muted strings, Énée cites la pudique Diane—the modest Diana—goddess of the hunt, who revealed herself to her human lover Endymion.

Speaking in the third person, Didon's reply, Par une telle nuit le fils de Cythérée acuellit froidement la tendresse envirée de la reine Didon—On such a night the son of Cytherea [another name for Venus; she is referring to and teasing Énée] responded coldly to the passionate love of Queen Dido—which of course he has not. His playfully chivalrous reply is that obtint de lui sa peine le plus tendre pardon—he gladly gave her his most tender forgiveness. This exchange takes place over a fervent six-note falling figure dominated by the clarinets that repeats through this passage. The composer instructs that the final iteration of the refrain be sung Avec exaltation—with exaltation—and here the vocal lines overlap closely and sweetly. Soon, they are instructed to sing more quietly, as the duet winds down, they ask: Blonde Phoebé . . .souriez à l'immortel amour—Golden Phoebe [goddess of the moon] . . . smile on our immortal love—though of course, ironically, their "immortal love" will soon end; even so, they leave the stage embracing.

A ray of moonlight falls on Énée's armor, which is resting against une colonne tronqué—a broken column. Berlioz shifts keys from the rich-sounding one in which the duet was set to one of the bleakest in the classical harmonic vocabulary; the heavy brass and sternly unmuted strings now dominate the orchestral sound. Mercure appears, striking the shield twice with his wand; that somber tone is portrayed by the tamtam, a huge gong. Three times, he reiterates that immutable demand of the gods for Énée: Italie! And the act ends in shivers, shudders, and gloom.

While comparisons with Wagner's Tristan and Isolde are inevitable, Didon and Énée belong to our shared Greco-Roman mythology, with a healthy dose of Shakespeare blended in, adding a note of courtly Renaissance artifice in the lovers' final exchange where Didon teases Énée, who responds chivalrously. Of course, the long duet from act 2 of *Tristan und Isolde* is one of the great moments in opera, music, and Western culture, deeply erotic if a bit murky in its ideas. Great on its own very different terms, Berlioz's conception is lighter, tighter, even joyous, at least until Mercure makes his proclamation.

Complex and powerful, act 5 is set in three scenes. In the first, some Trojans express their longing for home while others say they like Carthage; but Panthée and other leaders hear the spirits calling them to Italy. Having told Didon that he's leaving, Énée is surprised at her fury. The ghosts of Troy remind him of his mission, and he prepares to depart. Didon arrives and rebukes him. In the second scene, Didon asks Anna to plead with Énée to stay. The Trojans sail; Didon resolves to die. In

Les Troyens, Virgil (. . . and Shakespeare) 141

the closing scene, priests of Pluton (Pluto, the god of the dead) set up a pyre, at which Didon predicts that Carthage will one day be revenged. Didon stabs herself, then dies. As the Carthaginians curse the Trojans, a vision of a triumphant Rome—the second Troy—appears.

This violent and tragic act opens gently with a pathos-laden moment for Hylas, a Trojan sailor, who sings from a masthead of his longing for the home he'll never see again. Vallon sonore—O echoing vale—displays the composer's melodic phrasing at its most flexible and free, perhaps unexpectedly in this blended lullaby and prayer. Set in three verses, this lyrical lament opens with a rocking rhythm set by the lower strings, joined by the clarinets. Hylas, a tenor needing a wide range, expresses longing for his homeland. His line rises in pain: Je m'en allais chantant, hélas—I used to wander singing, alas!—away from the rocking rhythm but exquisitely decorated by woodwinds and rich-sounding cellos. The singer's line drops for the prayer to the sea that ends every verse: Berce mollement sur ton sein sublime, ô puissante mer, enfant de Dindyme—Rock gently on your generous breast, mighty sea, child of Dindyma [mother of the gods in some Greek myths]. The composer always breaks to 6/8 meter for the closing line, giving a fervent quality to Hylas's prayer. At the conclusion of the second verse, Fraîche ramée, retraite aimée—Cool, green branches, cherished retreat—the orchestra rumbles below with a hint of a sea-storm. In the final verse, Hylas's song is commented on pithily by two Trojan guards, one who notes that he's dreaming of his homeland; the second replies: which he won't see again. (The watchmen will soon have a short, great duet of their own.) This great aria ends with Hylas's voice trailing off as he sings himself to sleep.

An ensemble in recitative for Panthée, Préparez tout—Get everything ready—Trojan soldiers, and Trojan ghosts moves the plot along. Panthée sings that Énée has told Didon that he must depart, and that she is furious and inconsolable. The Trojans agree that Signes effrayants—Ghastly portents—have been warning them, as a small offstage chorus calls "Italie" softly but distinctly. The Trojans react: Dieux vengeurs! C'est leur voix!—Avenging gods, that is their voice!—then mutter that they can no longer delay. Musically, the scene is interesting for a recurring syncopated figure for lower strings that hints at the spectral while making an effective link to the next number. At once charming and serious, the brief duet for the watchmen who just commented on Hylas's lullaby now complain as they march about the still-rumored departure and how much they like life in Carthage. Unlike Énée, these men emphatically do not hear the call of glory: Par Bacchus, ils sont fous avec leur "Italie"—By Bacchus, they're mad with their "Italy." Both have Carthaginian girlfriends and appreciate the generosity of their hosts, as they exchange their short lines to a delicately phrased, nocturnal march directly descended from those in *L'Enfance du Christ*. Bassoons and pizzicato strings carry the march rhythm, while woodwinds, notably the clarinets, soften the orchestral textures. One quiets the other as their chief approaches.

Highly agitated, Énée spills his anxieties and misgivings in a headlong, densely packed dramatic recitative: Inutiles regrets! Je dois quitter Carthage!—Futile regrets! I must leave Carthage! This otherwise fearless warrior vacillates between shock at thoughts of Didon's rage at his announcement, regret at having to leave and his own inescapable awareness that he must—En vain ai-je parlé des prodiges sans nombre me rappelant l'ordre des dieux—In vain I told her of countless portents which remind me of the gods' command—ending his narrative on this potent image: Son regard la terrible éloquence—The terrible power of her look. The accompaniment hurtles along, with the orchestra echoing Énée's phrasing.

The recitative leads directly into a two-part aria in which Énée expresses his several regrets slowly and lyrically, followed by a turnaround as he decides to see her once more to thank her and apologize again. This dual form, in which a quick-tempo passage where the performer shows resolution and gets to show off vocally follows a display of skill at portraying a tender emotion, is an ancient operatic convention. It has had a long life (see "Glitter and be Gay" from Bernstein's *Candide* of 1956) and still works surprisingly well.

Énée's aria Ah, quand viendra l'instant des suprêmes adieux—But, ah, when the moment comes for the last farewell—opens with a sighing figure for the woodwinds which Énée picks up as the opening phrase of his melody. Two-note sighs for the violins sharpen his expression of pain and regret. Énée is also accompanied by a French horn that adds a masculine tone to the accompanying ensemble. Berlioz also works in delicate major-to-minor key shifts to emphasize certain words and in turn Énée's unease, such as de cette douleur indignée—of her indignant grief. In the fast passage that follows, the mature Berlioz displays both freedom and restraint, as these passages (called cabalettas in Italian operas) can be clattery and coarse. Slight hesitations of phrasing and tempo express the confusion of a man of action who's uncharacteristically uncertain. En un dernier naufrage puissé-je périr—May I drown in a shipwreck—is quick and quite challenging vocally, scattered with many high notes.

But Énée is stopped dead in his tracks by the appearance of Trojan ghosts, including those of Priam, Chorèbe, Hector, and Cassandre, each veiled and crowned with flames. They call out to him in turn to leave at once: Plus de retards! Pas une heure!—No more delay! Not an hour! In a high-set reply that expresses his terror, Énée cries out that he must yield to their demands, and that J'immole Didon, en détournant les yeux—Dido must be sacrificed, without a glance from me. Berlioz's music for this short but effective scene follows mid-nineteenth-century operatic procedure with a standard, spooky harmonic scheme of which there are countless examples from Weber's *Der Freischutz* to Verdi's *Macbeth*. But his orchestration is really what makes the scene work, from the chord for the violins set in icy, whistling harmonics to the shivering string tremolo played on the bridges of the instruments.

A terrified Énée now cries out to the Trojan chiefs in a quick-tempo call that they must leave, and now, finally taking up the cry of "Italie" himself. His orders (Coupez les câbles, il est temps!—Cut the cables, the time has come!) are barked out to a frantic setting of the Trojan March that's broken into a jerky, short-long rhythm making him seem more puppet than hero, reinforced by powerful blasts for the heavy brass that suggest the gods' imperative. He calls for Ascagne and the others to be roused, and, toward the end, over an accompaniment of pulsing woodwind triplets underpinned by a beautiful rising phrase for the strings, he cries out a passionate, if self-justifying farewell to Didon: Pour la mort des héros je te suis infidèle!—For a hero's death I forsake you!

Didon enters, majestic in her fury, as the once loving pair have an angry, fast-moving duet in which she spits her contempt but also cannot hide her desperation: Tu pars? Sans remords?—You are going? Without remorse? Énée tries to explain, J'ai trop tardé . . . des dieux les ordres souverains—I have delayed to long . . . the gods' sovereign command. Although he cannot stay, Énée claims to love Didon—Jusqu'au dernier jour—Until the end of time. The strings express the sting of her emotions, as chords for the woodwinds capture his futile attempts to soothe her. The tonality is shifted and pace slowed a bit as Didon tries to coax Énée by reminding him of the care she took of Ascagne when he went to war (Encore, si de ta foi j'avais un tendre gage . . . un fils d' Énée—Yet I had a tender pledge of your trust . . . Aeneas's son). But as the Trojan March rings brassily from offstage, Énée claims passionately enough: Je pars et je vous aime—I go, and I love you; to which Didon replies in a phrase of tremendous intensity, Ne sois pas plus longtemps par mes cris arrêté, monstre de piété!—Do not let my tears delay you longer, monster of piety!—cursing him and his gods to slashing chords for the woodwinds and strings, then storming offstage. Énée and the Trojans set sail to the strains of the March, stiffly phrased, which we are made to hear again as a fateful summons rather a triumphant declaration.

Didon's grief, private and public, alternate in the opera's last two scenes. Set in Didon's chamber, the penultimate scene between Didon, Anna, and Narbal opens with a beautiful falling phrase, echoed by the cellos, set over a pulsing rhythm that captures the queen's despairing weeping. Va ma soeur, l'implorer . . . l'orgeuil a fui—Sister, go, entreat him . . . my pride has fled—she asks Anna, who replies that she herself is to blame, but also that Son départ est inévitable . . . et pourtant il vous aime—Nothing can stop his going . . . and yet he loves you. Grasping even at this false hope, she asks Anna and Narbal to go and plead with Énée, who is leaving as this takes place: Mais va, ma soeur, allez, Narbal, le supplier pour qu'il m'accorde encore quelques jours seulement—But go, sister, and you, Narbal, beg him to grant just a few days more—as Berlioz shifts to a flickering major harmony that captures the pathos of her hope. Brief but lovely, this musically gorgeous scene captures our pity for this spurned lover.

A cry from an offstage chorus reports that the Trojans have sailed. Didon begins a monologue that alternates rage and despair. First, she cries out to Anna, Iopas, and Narbal to send her fighters after the Trojans: Courbez-vous sur les rames—Bend to the oars. These lines are set to an accompaniment that's spare but of great impetus. Soon, though, she realizes that this is futile: Que dis-je? Impuissante fureur!—What am I saying? Impotent rage! Didon works herself into fury once again, referring bitterly to Énée as cette âme pieuse—that pious soul—for his insistence on obeying his gods, finally saying that she should have had Ascagne cooked and served up as un hideux festin—a hideous banquet—for Énée; this of course, a moral low point for this noble character. Finally, though, to a strange and somber phrase for low-lying flutes and clarinets Didon orders the others to summon the priests of Pluton; she proposes to burn all tokens of Énée—souvenirs détestés—hateful memorials—in a pyre. Narbal perceives a worrisome change in Didon's manner, asking Anna to stay with her sister, but Didon orders them all out: Je suis reine et j'ordonne—I am Queen and I command it—and the others clear the stage for her great confession and farewell.

Didon's scene is broken into two roughly equal parts, beginning with a recitative. The instrumental introduction depicts her frantic despair in rushing phrases as she cries out, Ah! Je vais mourir!—Ah, I am going to die!—this resolution of course the change Narbal observed. The tempo slows and a somber, deep-set line for the clarinet intones a phrase that recurs throughout in punctuation. She hopes Énée will see the glow of her funeral pyre, wherever he is, and that Peut-être il pleurera sur mon affreux destin—Perhaps he will weep at my pitiful fate. Her vocal line rises, then sinks as she describes the fall of her soul: L'emporte en l'éternelle nuit—Bears it down to everlasting night. She then pleads in another passionate falling phrase with Énée's mother: Vénus, rends-moi ton fils—Venus, give me back your son—then answers herself that was the inutile prière d'un coeur qui se déchire—futile prayer of a heart torn asunder.

Relatively brief but dense and certainly to the point, Adieu, fière cite—Farewell, proud city—is a resigned Didon's lullaby set in a major key. Again, the clarinet and other woodwinds dominate the accompaniment of this gentle passage where she bids farewell, in order, to her city, her sister (Ma tendre soeur), her people, the shore that welcomed them. Then she sings Adieu, beau ciel d'Afrique—Farewell, fair skies of Africa—and the stars she gazed on (with Énée, though she does not mention him) on those nuits d'ivresse—nights of rapture. Berlioz creates a potent lyrical climax that's all the more effective for its restraint, with a single iteration, now set in Didon's desolate recollection, of the great melody of the love duet. Her aria ends on Ma carrière et est finie—My career is ended—another line reminiscent of Shakespeare ("Othello's occupation's gone!" in act 3, scene 3) on a phrase that rises melodically but to a desolate harmony, followed by shuddering strings and somber chords for the orchestra.

The final scene of *Les Troyens* is set in Didon's garden by the sea, where a large pyre has been set up. Opening with a dark-hued march for the priests of Pluton summoned in the prior scene, the queen enters with Anna and Narbal. Set to a steady beat, and with woodwinds, brass, and percussion initially dominating the orchestral textures, the priests pray: Dieux d'oubli, au coeur blessé rendez la force et le repos—Gods of oblivion, restore strength and peace to the wounded heart. As witnesses to Didon's intimate confession, the audience knows of her imminent suicide. In fury and to a more animated accompaniment that includes upward rushing gestures for the strings, Anna and Narbal ask the gods to grant Énée un obscur trépas—an inglorious death—adding vivid images of him as pâture aux dévorants oiseaux—carrion for birds of prey. Their dramatic, irregular phrases contrast with the cool steadiness of the priests' march, which returns to end the passage and in which they then join.

Didon enters, to a quieting phrase: C'en est fait . . . achevons le pieux sacrifice . . . Je sens rentrer le calme dans mon coeur—All is over . . . Let us finish the holy sacrifice . . . I feel peace returning to my heart. The somber march theme returns over a pulsing accompaniment that suggests higher emotion, followed by gentle flutes and clarinets, interrupted more and more frequently by figures for the strings and brass that rush tensely ahead. Didon contemplates Énée's gifts and the sword and shield he left behind in his rush to leave; the bed they shared is also on the pyre. She works herself into greater grief as she considers all these tokens of their love, predicting: Mon souvenir vivra parmi les âges—My memory will live through the ages. In visionary tone, she predicts a great Carthaginian warrior, Annibal—Hannibal—who will revenge her on the descendants of Trojans. Crying fiercely, C'est ainsi qu'il convient de descendre aux enfers—Thus it's fitting to go down to the shades below!—she then stabs herself with Énée's sword.

Operatic cries of dismay follow as the big also chorus also enters, asking, Est'il vrai? Jour d'horreur!—Is it true? Day of horror! Didon calls out to a swooning Anna. But as another vision of Rome triumphant appears cinematically in the background, Didon realizes: Des destins ennemis . . . Carthage périra—The fates are against us . . . Carthage will perish—then utters the name of the conquering city and empire as her dying words. In what's called L'Imprécation—The Curse—all Carthage swears haine éternelle à la race d'Énée—undying hatred for the race of Aeneas. This short chorus in which the Carthaginians chant that they and their descendants will fight, is set ironically to the thundering Trojan March, amplified by harps, which here as always add a sense of climactic rapture.

While we all may sense that the Trojan March must somehow form the musical ending of *Les Troyens*, how well it actually works here is debatable. Plenty of operatic endings are as contrived as this and many even more so, but this also feels cluttered and hectic, as though the composer had too much in the way of words, ideas and music to cram in—not unlike *Benvenuto Cellini*. In any case, the present ending seems to be an improvement on an earlier, even more overworked plan; and clearly the composer had some difficulty with how to end the opera.[81]

Summer Nights

Berlioz composed songs over the entire course of his career, with most collected and published in 1865 as "Thirty-Three Melodies." Among these, the six that had already been extracted, orchestrated, and organized as *Les Nuits d'été*—Summer Nights—may be the greatest, and are by far the best known and most influential. The poems set were taken from an anthology titled *La Comédie de la Mort*—The Comedy of Death—by Théophile Gautier, a poet, journalist, and friend of the composer's. The six deal, like many in the song literature, with love, its loss, and death. They seem not to have come together initially as the suite that is the final product, but over time solidified in the composer's mind as a whole work, in his brilliant ordering. The title, unspecific but evocative, is also his.[82] The original version, for voice and piano, has been superseded by Berlioz's orchestrations, which weren't all done at once. Their performance history is complex, even a bit tortured. But *Les Nuits d'été* is so extraordinarily fine, approaching perfection, that questions and details about its creation and versions adapted for singers the composer knew have faded to insignificance.

The songs that make up *Les Nuits d'été* are:

1. *Villanelle* ("Villanelle," a type of lyric poem)
2. *Le Spectre de la Rose* ("The Ghost of the Rose")
3. *Sur les Lagunes (Lamento)* ("On the Lagoons," subtitled "Lament")
4. *Absence* ("Absence")
5. *Au Cimetière (Clair de Lune)* ("At the Cemetery," subtitled "Moonlight")
6. *L'Île inconnue* ("The Unknown Island")

As some of the titles suggest, the subjects and tones of several poems are gloomy, as is Berlioz's treatment. Two, *Villanelle* and *L'Île inconnue*, are cheerful, if, as we'll see, ambiguously so, and two fall between. *Le Spectre de la Rose* is melancholy; and *Absence*, while filled with painful longing, doesn't express outright despair. That's the effect of *Sur les Lagunes*, a grief-stricken lament, and darkest of the set, with the morbid exercise that is *Au Cimetière* a close second. "Their arrangement, with the airy, major-key songs at either end and *Absence* in more or less the dramatic center, framed by the two most somber moments, is demonstrably purposeful, for we know the original order of the songs to have been changed to that effect."[83] The cycle as it has come down to us has the clear feeling of passing from the naïve happiness of *Villanelle* through crises of increasing gravity, coming out at the end with the sense, in *L'Île inconnue*, that life goes on.

The songs seem to have been written in 1840 and 1841; but "We know less about *Les Nuits d'été* and its genesis than almost any other major work of his . . . The songs are not mentioned in the correspondence of 1840-41, the presumed period of their composition."[84] The original version is for voice and piano, which, as we know, Berlioz did not play; so he must have had help with that. (Certainly, he counted many great pianists, including Chopin and Liszt, as friends.) The originals, apparently conceived with no singer in mind, are scored for a high voice, perhaps mezzo-soprano or tenor, but clearly not a bass or baritone. Two of the later, orchestrated versions (the second and third, *Le Spectre de la Rose* and *Sur les Lagunes*) are also in different keys from the originals.

The reason for these changes is that some early performers, to whom Berlioz dedicated the orchestrated versions of the songs, were of different vocal categories, requiring transposition of the music to more comfortable keys than the original, generic settings with piano. Transposition, where music is shifted whole from one key to another, is a common practice for singers, whose voices sit better in certain registers, often different from those in which the music is originally written. If you listen to recordings by three great singers (Janet Baker, Régine Crespin, and Victoria de los Angeles) performing *Au Cimetière*, you'll immediately hear that they sing in different keys. There's much discussion among musicologists and critics as to whether this is acceptable; they also debate which version is the most authentic. Perhaps the best versions are those by intelligent singers with beautiful voices, as concerns over authenticity somehow disappear in the face of a convincing performance.

Recordings by the sopranos mentioned here—all beautiful in their way—were made in the 1950s and '60s. Some later recordings try to use the voice categories specified by Berlioz in his dedications of the orchestral versions of the songs; to me, these never quite come together. It's also good to keep in mind that native speakers of French (Crespin among these three sopranos) deliver the text more naturally and easily, which isn't really surprising. Crespin's otherwise peerless 1963 recording inexplicably switches the order of *Absence* and *Sur les Lagunes*. There's a fine performance by the Belgian bass-baritone José van Dam with piano that, as the original version, is well worth hearing. And by the way, it's transposed to fit van Dam's vocal range.

Berlioz's orchestrations, mostly for woodwinds, French horns, strings, and a harp in *Le Spectre de la Rose*, are light, foreshadowing the late-period transparency of *Béatrice et Bénédict*. His focus on the clarity of the delivery of the text is paramount and astonishing in the degree of his sensitivity to hints and shades of meaning. The relatively small forces needed for performance have made *Les Nuits d'été* one of the composer's best-known works. Those who find Berlioz sprawling might be surprised at how tight these six numbers are, without an ounce of fat; and listeners who think he's bombastic or blustery should listen to these studies in subtlety.

Les Nuits d'été belongs to the formal category called song cycles, which means that the songs are grouped and assembled by the composer. Some song cycles, such as Schubert's *Die schöne Müllerin*—The Miller's Beautiful Daughter—tell a story; most, including *Les Nuits d'été*, don't, but still achieve unity of subject and tone. Love and loss are the most common subjects, both of narrative song cycles, like Schubert's; they are also the topics of Gautier's poems and of Berlioz's cycle. Two of the greatest song cycles, Beethoven's *An die Ferne Geliebte*—To the Distant Beloved—and Schumann's *Dichterliebe*—A Poet's Love—are so tightly woven musically and in subject as to feel like narratives; but Beethoven's consists only of six poetic reflections on love and loss. In Schumann's extraordinary set, sixteen poems by Heinrich Heine reflect the anger and disappointment of a jilted lover, but it's also not a narrative.

The six of *Les Nuits d'été*, while also about love, separation, and loss, are revolutionary because they're orchestrated. This seems to be the first song cycle with orchestral accompaniment, and, as such, it has been deeply influential. Other important orchestral cycles soon followed, including Wagner's *Wesendonck Lieder*, the subject of which is unrequited love, and show great stylistic unity. They're also significant as studies for *Tristan und Isolde*. Richard Strauss's *Vier Letzte Lieder*—Four Last Songs—reflect on life and mortality with opulent vocal and orchestral treatment. The best known and most popular song cycle these days is probably Mahler's *Das Lied von der Erde*—The Song of the Earth—six Germanic-orientalist meditations on beauty and its transience, but which, again, tells no story. Mahler composed four song cycles as well as many lieder that represent some of his best work. There are many more examples to be cited, but Ravel's *Shéhérazade* is another magnificent cycle from the same era of high orientalism in European music as *Das Lied von der Erde*. Ravel's gorgeous song triptych is integrated by its sensual mood rather than subject.

In opera, we generally know which character is singing. But in song, that information is not always as clear, though it's just as important to determine the persona speaking in the lyric; listeners need to figure out the point of view that's being expressed. Often, as in fiction, it's by an outside narrator, whether it's a narrative, reflective, or as with some lyrics from the mid-nineteenth century and later, abstract. However beautiful the music itself or the voice delivering it, full appreciation of the composer's and performer's art require that the listener orient him- or herself about this. In most cases the poetic persona is obvious. Of *Les Nuits d'été*, only one number, *L'Île inconnue*, might confuse, because it's a dialogue between a man and woman. In solo performance, a skilled singer will characterize both without difficulty.

The opening song, *Villanelle*, takes its title from a poetic form with six verses, which are typically shown as three in printed texts of this poem. Each of Gautier's verses are actually subtly broken in the middle to mimic the six-verse form. The original villanelles, from Italy, dating approximately to the fifteenth century, referred to a villa—a country house—and often had a rustic character, which Gautier captures with straightforward charm. In the first verse, the generic rustic narrator asks his girl to walk with him through the woods; in the second, he praises spring and love; in the third, he describes wildlife they'll see and their return, hand in hand. Throughout, the poet's imagery is as conventional as it might be, with dew, flowers, blackbirds and other fauna. Although Berlioz's setting is bright, capturing the poem's cheerful affect, the composer can't resist some musical ironies in the form of tugs on the accompaniment and unexpected melodic trajectories.

The music opens, brightly, almost chirpily, with a plain A-major chord, tapped out by the flutes, oboes, and clarinets, in steady, detached eighth notes. The singer enters almost immediately, but even her first line, which ends on froids—cold—moves unexpectedly to a note outside the key and already in another tonality (G-minor), far from A Major. The cellos add a five-note falling figure that reinforces G-minor, not A-major, while the woodwinds continue to chug steadily away. Keep in mind that we're only about ten seconds into the first song, the simplest of the six; the composer is not only sensitive to hints of ambiguities in the words, but adds his own freely, as well. For example, the second line, Sous nos pieds égrenant les perles—Beneath our feet pearls of dew—contains harmonic shifts as a bouncing pizzicato figure for cellos and double basses returns to a more playful mood; but the singer's line pulls away persistently from the home key. With the words Nous irons écouter les merles siffler—We'll go hear the blackbirds sing—the bassoons enter with an elegant imitation of the bird's song that returns in the second and third verses.

In the second verse, violas and cellos imitate the singer's line closely and playfully; the second line of the verse, Et l'oiseau, satinant son aile—And the bird, smoothing his wing—their contribution is strongly accented, as the violins join in grace notes and trills that suggest birdlike movement. At the end of the verse, Berlioz instructs the singer to pause for breath before the final word, Toujours—Forever—uttered by the generic country girl to her generic beau.

The third verse, beginning Loin, bien loin égarant nos courses—Straying far from our path—contains the most surprises in the form of continual, dizzying harmonic oscillations. The steady chug of eighth notes now shifts to the violins and violas, as a low-lying clarinet joins the cellos and double basses in commentary that first seems ominous but which changes almost immediately to something more playful. As before, the vocalist's line moves in unexpected directions, often hitting a high point then drooping away.

Le Spectre de la Rose moves to a mood of gentle melancholy. Its text carries an old-fashioned and elaborate poetic conceit: a fading rose worn by a young woman attending her first ball the night before has died the most enviable of deaths, with the rose, or more properly, its ghost, as the narrating persona. The form of Berlioz's musical setting is "through-composed," meaning the words are set straight through, without recurring thematic ideas, unlike the regular verse of *Villanelle*. Notable for a dreamlike, proto-cinematic feel, *Le Spectre de la Rose* shows some of the composer's most characteristic stylistic fingerprints. Although it has the feel of a slow waltz, it's actually set in his favorite 9/8 beat to a melody so long and languid that it may better be considered an extended melodic structure.

Gautier's text will seem corny (or worse) to modern sensibilities, but the composer treats it at a distance, making for a flawless, indeed timeless merging of words and music. In the opening verse of three, the ghost of the rose addresses the young woman, who's waking on the morning after her first ball. In the second verse, the spectral rose says its soul as perfume will remain with her for a while; in the last verse, the young woman is told that to die on her breast was a fate to be envied by kings.

To a quiet opening for strings, the flutes and clarinets sing out the expansive melody, to which the violins add a six-note spinning figure that plays an ever-widening role through the song. The string section plays with mutes throughout the opening verse, creating a cool, slightly distant sound. The spinning figure grows into a continuous accompaniment for the violas as the singer enters, her line set low and deeply expressive. The violins add delicate trills, suggesting perhaps some recalled excitement from the night before. As in all these songs, the melody and harmonic accompaniment take unexpected turns, as in the composer's setting of the phrase Des pleurs d'argent de l'arrosoir—

With silvery tears from being watered—from the second line of the poem, which drifts away from the home key. Thanks to the spaciousness and gentle mood of *Le Spectre de la Rose,* such changes come across more subtly than in some of the later, darker-hued numbers, but it's just as richly shaded as any. Toward the end of the first verse, pulsing woodwinds join the accompaniment, artfully preparing the way for more animated rhythmic setting of the second verse, O toi, qui de ma mort fus cause—O you, cause of my death.

Plucked strings in faster-moving but still quiet sixteenth notes back the singer; these move to detached notes for the flutes and clarinets. The composer breaks their pattern and that of the singer to create a panting effect as the vocal line, heretofore so fluid, separates into falling, detached notes on Mais ne crains rien je ne réclame ni messe ni De Profundis—But do not be afraid, I demand neither Mass nor De Profundis. (The Latin words refer to a Roman Catholic prayer for the dead.) The harp enters, first in delicate accompaniment, but soon in a thicker, more impassioned contribution alongside the full orchestra, as strings, now unmuted, reach the song's climax on J'arrive du paradis—I come from paradise—which are condensed and repeated ecstatically five times. The dynamics, at a gentle *forte* (loud), reinforce the passage's climactic quality.

The composer treats the last verse as a pullback that moves toward a quiet ending. The orchestral texture is thinned to trembling stings for its opening line, Mon destin fut digne d'envie—My fate was enviable. A bit of punctuation from the woodwinds and French horns add a bit more color, as limping figures for strings take over the accompaniment. A solo clarinet in harmony accompanies the singer for the closing, clinching line: Ci-gît une rose, que tous les rois vont jalouser—Here lies a rose which every king will envy. It's worth listening for the care with which the composer sets the last three notes of the song, for the string section. All but the double basses are bowed while the basses are softly plucked.

Sur les Lagunes—On the Lagoons—carries the subtitle *Lamento,* which, translates from Italian, not French, as "Lament." Expressing comprehensibly human pain, this is the darkest moment of *Les Nuits d'été.* The narrator-persona is a sailor whose beloved has died, and he expresses his grief in gloomy, often morbid imagery over three verses, each of which ends with the refrain, Que mon sort est amer! Ah, sans amour s'en aller sur la mer!—Bitter is my lot! Ah, to go loveless to sea! *Sur les Lagunes* stands among the greatest and most gripping expressions of grief in music

Berlioz sets this tragic poem in a freely conceived through-composed setting, whose oppressive nature is clear right from the opening, in which a French horn and the violins utter a moaning half-step interval that will be repeated thirteen times, dominating the orchestral accompaniment, and acting as the musical motto for the song. The violas, cellos, and double basses play a rocking, barcarolle-like figure that suggests oceanic movement. But little time is wasted, as the vocalist, singing low in her range, enters after only one dense introductory measure. Ma belle amie est morte, je pleurerai toujours—My beloved is dead, I shall weep forever—is her opening line, which although in a narrow melodic range is still more free than that of the accompaniment. By her third line, Dans le ciel, sans m'attendre, elle s'en retourna—She returned to heaven without waiting for me—the composer inserts quick shifts from minor to major, perhaps to suggest heaven, just mentioned, but also to demonstrate the depth of the narrator's despair; these few oscillations flicker and are gone. The first line of the refrain (Ah, que mon sort est amer) is set to a tight melodic phrase in the singer's middle range over a motionless chord for the lower strings; the closing line (Ah! Sans amour . . .) starts more dramatically on a relatively high note with a falling scale in detached notes, trailed by the clarinets, bassoons, and French horns.

Berlioz merges the second and third verses of Gautier's poem with consummate skill, building to its climactic passage, with a falling away at the end not unlike that of *Le Spectre de la Rose*. The first line of the second verse, La blanche créature est couchée au cercueil—The pale beauty is lying in her coffin—over pulsing woodwinds, with a high-set French horn moaning out another half-step, here in a major key, which still offers no relief, pulling almost continually to minor inflections and, indeed, other tonalities: tout me paraît en deuil—everything seems to me to be in mourning). Now the singer expresses more animation but also more agitation as rising violins and flutes imitate the mourning dove, climaxing musically in a pain-racked outburst, Pleure, pleure, et songe à l'absent—Weeps and dreams of her missing mate. The refrain is set to stark, disjointed harmonies.

In an extraordinary vocal challenge, Berlioz opens the third verse, Sur moi la nuit immense s'étend comme un linceuil—Over me the immense night is spread like a shroud—with an eerie low E on the last note for singers who can summon it, which some, like Baker and Crespin achieve; others are provided with an easier alternate. So tightly woven is the composer's treatment here that any sense of regularity of the verse setting is obliterated. With the next passage, opening with Je chante ma romance que le ciel entend seul—I sing my song which only the heavens hear—Berlioz finds the musical and emotional climax. The vocal line breaks out into grief expressed in wider intervals but shorter phrases, as the strings move to tremolandos for the climactic line, Je n'aimerais jamais une femme autant qu'elle—I will never love a woman as much as her—which Berlioz breaks in two. Its first half concludes the rising expressions of despair; after the flutes and clarinets compress a spinning figure in preparation for the song's climactic phrase. Woodwinds and singer then share an arching phrase that is the spinning phrase for woodwinds just completed, but where every note is emphasized in agony. The moaning half-step is brought back immediately as the long, dark postlude based only the words of the refrain, begins. It's worth listening for the contrary motion of the clarinets and cellos as they fall against the rising vocal line on the final iteration of sur la mer—on the sea; and there are two expressions of inarticulate despair for the singer, as the violas, cellos, and double basses continue their flowing movement to the end.

Absence, the title of fourth song, has the same meaning—if a different pronunciation—in French as in English. This slow-tempo meditation on love and separation, which stands as "more or less the dramatic center"[85] of *Les Nuits d'été*, has a grandeur that sets it apart in character from the other songs. (Although all six differ completely from one another.) It's set in a clear strophic form, where repeated phrases—the refrain—are set to the same music; these alternate with verses of a different character, which can be shown schematically as ABABA. The refrain (A), heard three times, is so deliberate as to seem motionless. The alternating verses (B), which intervene twice, move somewhat faster. The clear structure of *Absence* may make it a bit easier than its companions to grasp as one gets to know *Les Nuits d'été*. Jacques Barzun describes *Absence* as "another expression of the same feeling of void, but the tremendous call to the departed lover springs from a loneliness that has once been shared and is now twice bitter."[86]

More than just a sigh set to music, the rising opening phrase, for the full orchestra is an expression of purest longing, which the singer who enters immediately after, copies. Reviens, reviens, ma bien-aimée—Come back, come back, my beloved—is the opening line of the refrain. Berlioz fills the phrasing with carefully gauged adjustments to the dynamics, as well as pauses and extensions of note values that create a breadth and stillness that demand considerable control from the singer. The second line, Comme une fleur loin du soleil—Like a flower far from the sun—is rendered in a lovely, pensive phrase; and the clincher, Loin de ton sourire vermeil—Far from your ruby smile—opens passionately on the highest note in the song, then falls; the composer accompanies this phrase with a richly harmonized but quiet cadence for the full orchestra.

A slowly descending scale for the French horns and cellos open the first verse in a slightly faster tempo and a more troubled mood. That descent sets the tone for the text, Entre nos coeurs quelle distance—What distance between our hearts—with more pain, in pulsing, richly harmonized strings, and an outburst on the last line, O grands désirs inapaisés—O great, unassuaged desires—that's also set to a falling phrase. The refrain, which follows, is repeated exactly. The second verse, D'ici là-bas—Between here and there—resembles but doesn't precisely copy the first musically, but deepens its sense of longing. The composer punctuates the final iteration of the refrain with high-set sighs for muted strings.

As gloomy as *Sur les Lagunes* but in a different way is the penultimate number, *Au Cimetière* (Track 8). This strange but beautiful lament also carries the pictorial subtitle *Clair de lune*, which, of course, means "moonlight." This eerie number depicts a graveyard at and after twilight, where the fear of the dead of being forgotten is described, a subject far removed from normal experience. How well the rational, worldly Berlioz succeeds may surprise.

The six verses of *Au Cimetière* receive a strophic setting in which the first and second are merged musically. Verses 5 and 6 inexactly repeat 1 and 2, with the combined 3 and 4 being different, with the effect being that of an ABA form. The composer's conception and execution are extremely delicate. The orchestration, for flutes, clarinets, and muted strings, is light but clear. The singer is instructed at the opening to sing "à un quart de voix"—that is, at quarter-voice, or very softly, which is much more difficult physically than singing loud or even moderately loud, and which certainly doesn't come naturally to vocalists as performers. Berlioz never raises the singer's dynamic level, even in the song's climactic passage. Its melody is hauntingly beautiful, but what really makes this song remarkable is how Berlioz creates an impression of monotony without actually becoming monotonous. He does this in several ways, one of which is to vary and ornament the thematic material. But his most effective method is to hold to one steady beat and pace for most of the song's six-minute length, while continually shifting the melodic shading and supporting harmony. These move together, creating a hesitant uncertainty in almost every measure. This technique effectively suggests the poem's imagery of a white tomb, a yew tree, night flowers and particularly the pale dove whose cooing seems like the lament of souls who fear being forgotten, all in fading light.

Au Cimetière opens with pulsing notes from the strings, after which the singer enters with the opening line: Connaissez-vous la blanche tombe, où flotte avec un son plaintif l'ombre d'un if?—Do you know the white tomb, where the shadow of a yew floats plaintively? The first four measures stay in the home key, but in the fifth, on the word tombe, the accompaniment gently shifts harmony; in the tenth bar, on plaintif, the vocal line also drifts. *Au Cimetière* is so dense with expressive changes like these that it could easily sustain a measure by measure examination, but there's no room in an overview like this. A few examples along the way will have to do; and you're advised to get to know this wonderful example of high-romantic spectral tone painting.

Flutes, clarinets, and cellos move downward on l'ombre d'un if—shadow of a yew—painting that image in muted tones. On the final words of the verse, Chante son chant—Sings its song—the flutes take up in the same softly pulsing rhythm a cooing phrase that carries through much of the song; in fact, it's repeated in a new harmony moments later in the second verse. Changes of harmony in the melodic line and its accompaniment grow more unstable through the second verse, leading to a potent return to the home key on L'ange amoureux—A lovesick angel. Although this line serves as the climax of the first two verses, Berlioz sternly marks the singer's part *pppp*—*pianississississimo*—extremely softly.

The third verse, On dirait que l'âme éveillée—You would think that the awakened soul—opens with a change in the accompaniment, which moves to notes that are half the length of what just preceded; but still continue the sense of steady pulsation. Orchestral textures are thinned considerably, though, to woodwinds and cellos. The vocal line is also reduced to a murmuring on a few notes, with less harmonic movement. With the fourth verse, Sur les ailes de la musique—On the wings of music—the vocal line ascends, as the accompaniment also intensifies its activity, moving toward the song's climax: On sent lentement revenir un souvenir—You feel a memory coming back slowly—as the woodwinds, depicting the act of recalling, rise briefly to express an ambiguous ecstasy. As noted, the singer is not allowed to increase her volume, and unstable harmonies return. To illustrate the words Dans un rayon tremblant—In a shimmering beam—the violins play in the strange, high, whistling tone called harmonics, as the woodwinds and cellos shift out of rhythm and harmony in a delicate tug-of-war.

The fifth and sixth verses return to the thematic material of the first two, but varied and seemingly bereft of what little energy those possessed. At first, only chords for the woodwinds interspersed with four-note falling figures for the violins and violas back the singer—Les belles de nuit, demi-closes—The night-flowers, half open. But eventually the pulsing quarter-notes that animated the opening return, as do the harmonic uncertainties. *Au Cimetière* ends on the tug-of-war between flutes, clarinets, and strings that decorated the end of the fourth verse. Because the closing words are Son chant plaintif—Its plaintive song—the composer omits the weird timbre of harmonics that depicted the previous imagery.

Track 9, *L'Île inconnue*—The Unknown Island—closes out the cycle brilliantly, yet again, ambiguously. Gautier's playfully ironic poem consists of a dialogue between a narrator-persona asking a young woman where she'd like him to take her, describing fantastical modes of transportation and exotic destinations that seemed impossibly remote in the 1830s. She gives a poignant yet wise answer that serves as the clinching line of the song, and of *Les Nuits d'été*. While fully alert to the ironies of the text, Berlioz finds the most cause for the expression of joy in this number, even reaching a moment of ecstasy toward the end.

Opening with a surging orchestral passage with a grand, swinging lilt, the singer asks the question, Dites, la jeune belle, où voulez-vous aller?—Tell me, my pretty girl, where do you want to go?—adding a tail, La voile enfle son aile, la brise va souffler—The sail spread its wings, the breeze is rising—that's the refrain to every verse of the song's modified strophic form. Bassoons and cellos scramble along below with a fast-moving figure in sixteenth notes that works better here than on the piano, where it sounds clumsy. (Opinions differ, but *L'Île inconnue* also seems to benefit most among its companions from expansion from the original keyboard accompaniment to orchestral treatment.) The questioning persona playfully lists the equipment on his fantasy ship: L'aviron est d'ivoire . . . j'ai pour lest un orange . . . pour voile un aile d'ange—The oar is of ivory . . . I have an orange for ballast . . . for the sail an angel's wing. This list and that in the next verse make *L'Île inconnue* a "list song," a surprisingly large category that contains more familiar gems than you might think.[87] The music fluidly reflects the whimsical nature of this text, and also in the destinations of the following verse. But as in so many of the earlier songs, the melody takes unpredictable turns, as does the harmony.

The persona then asks the girl where she'd like to sail, listing a far-flung assortment: la Baltique? Dans la mer Pacifique, dans l'île de Java?—the Baltic? The Pacific Ocean? To the island of Java? The refrain Dites-moi, la jeune belle is repeated, to which she replies, "Menez-moi," dit la belle . . .—Take me, she says—at last giving her rueful reply, to "la rive fidèle, où l'on aime toujours"—the shore of fidelity, where love lasts forever—which, of course, is why the island of the title is unknown. Six crisp chords from the flutes, oboes, and clarinets punctuate her next line, "Cette rive, ma chère, on ne la connaît guère, au pays des amours"—That shore, my darling, is hardly known in the land of love. These words are repeated again, accompanied by ecstatic laughter from the flutes and clarinets as the girl thinks how funny it all is; then the same words are repeated to a deeply melancholy phrase as she considers how sad. There's no more astonishing display of the composer's sensitivity to words and his skill at portraying their multiple meanings. The closing refrain returns to the voice of the male persona, who asks one last time, Où voulez-vous aller? La brise va souffler! But while the sealike rocking rhythm persists to the end, the quieting closing bars feel uncertain, uneasy, and ambiguous.

The next candidate for wider attention among the master's songs might well be *Neuf Mélodies irlandiases*—Nine Irish Songs. Set to lyrics by the Irish poet Thomas Moore, this early set (first published in 1830) is unlikely to knock *Les Nuits d'été* off its pedestal, but it's still worth hearing. One difficulty posed is the wide-ranging forces needed for performance, including four soloists, small chorus, pianist, and conductor. The audience, necessarily limited to Berlioz fanatics and the families and close friends of the performers, is small. Fortunately, it has been recorded by forces as described earlier, with four good singers led sympathetically by John Eliot Gardiner. The most immediately appealing are *Hélène*—Ellen—a charming duet for soprano and contralto, *La Belle Voyageuse*—The Beautiful Traveler—a lilting number scored for tenor but sung on the Gardiner-led recording by a contralto, and *L'Origine de la harpe*—The Origin of the Harp—a ballad in which Berlioz convincingly captures the tang of an Irish tune.

Listening to Berlioz

The biggest obstacle to hearing this composer and getting to know his style is the infrequency of live performances. With the exception of the *Symphonie fantastique* and the overtures, little else is programmed. His dramatic nature and vivid orchestral coloring simply can't be taken in on speakers, let alone on headphones. With that major condition in mind, the selection is a representative sampling across a varied and fascinating output. Naturally, the complete *Nuits d'été* would have been preferable to two of the six, but it was impossible to resist putting some on as an introduction to this extraordinary work. I wanted something from *L'Enfance du Christ*, but there wasn't room. Also missing is Nuit paisible et sereine, the glorious duet that concludes act 1 of *Béatrice et Bénédict*, so make sure to listen to that soon.

Although his scores are complex, demanding clarity in the interplay of themes and orchestration, without a hard to define dashing quality they can easily fall flat: another Berliozian paradox. I also wanted to mention briefly the conductors who are considered specialists. The British conductor Colin Davis, who died in 2013, is perhaps the most famous of them. He's one of the key figures in the Berlioz renaissance of the last century, probably doing more to expose the full scope of the composer's achievements than anyone. He performed everything many times and recorded most of the Berlioz oeuvre more than once. That said, I believe that the quality of Davis's conducting is inconsistent. Some seem slower in tempo than these energetic works require, and more dutiful than passionate. This is not uncommon, as many other conductors (Herbert von Karajan and Carlo Maria Giulini, for instance) slowed tempos noticeably over the course of their careers. This is not necessarily due to aging but because they sometimes learn to make their points with audiences, highlighting everyone's favorite moments by slowing and emphasizing. But that's not a good approach for Berlioz.

Leonard Bernstein wasn't considered a Berlioz specialist, but at his best he had the needed energy and focus, even in difficult works like the Requiem. Pierre Boulez, a successor of Bernstein's at the New York Philharmonic was also capable, leading the Cleveland Orchestra in an inspired, beautifully clear 2003 recording of *Roméo et Juliette*. My favorite among the dead is Charles Munch, the Frenchman who led the Boston Symphony Orchestra for thirteen years until his retirement in 1962. His Berlioz performances seem miraculous, always catching the right tone, moving effortlessly from lyrical to volcanic and back. This Berlioz specialist deserves as much credit as Davis, whom he preceded in reawakening interest in the composer. Munch recorded as much Berlioz as he could get away with when the composer wasn't so popular, including the overtures, the big symphonic works, the dramatic symphonies, *L'Enfance du Christ*, and the Requiem. Unfortunately, the operas weren't being produced back then for Munch to conduct, though as noted in chapter 9, he did record the Chasse royale et Orage—Royal Hunt and Storm—from *Les Troyens*. Anyway, you get the idea: listen to Munch.

Among living conductors, the American John Nelson leads the pack, with performances of high energy and clarity. His 2017 *Troyens* works better overall than Davis's first complete recording of the opera from 1969, though that certainly remains a landmark. Nelson's, featuring Joyce DiDonato as Didon, Michael Spyres as Énée, and Marie-Nicole Lemieux as Cassandre, simply moves better. Like Bernstein, not a specialist, Daniel Barenboim has shown the clarity and fire needed for Berlioz; Charles Dutoit is off and on, but when on can really get the job done. Although less active now, Seiji Ozawa, a successor of Munch's at the BSO, also has the touch, with one of the most beautiful recordings of *La Damnation de Faust* to his credit.

Notes

1. Winton Dean: *Les Troyens*, in *Essays on Opera*, p. 208.
2. Berlioz, *Memoirs*, trans. Cairns, p. 43.
3. Munch, *I Am a Conductor*, pp. 55–56.
4. Tovey, *Essays in Musical Analysis*, vol. 6, p. 45.
5. Rosen, *The Romantic Generation*, p. 555.
6. Ibid., pp. 542–568.
7. Ibid., pp. 542–543.
8. Berlioz, *Memoirs*, p. 107.
9. Ibid., p. 108.
10. Peter Bloom, ed. *The Cambridge Companion to Berlioz*. Bloom, *Berlioz and Wagner*, p. 243.
11. Berlioz, *Memoirs*, p. 98.
12. Ibid., pp. 114–115.
13. Ibid. p. 201.
14. D. F. Tovey, *Essays in Musical Analysis*, vol. 4, p. 79.
15. Quoted in Holoman, p. 206
16. Diana Bickley, "The concert overtures," in *The Cambridge Companion to Berlioz*, ed. Bloom, p. 72.
17. Ibid., p. 69.
18. Ibid., p. 73.
19. Ibid., p. 77.
20. Tovey, *Illustrative Music*, pp. 82–86.
21. Cairns, vol. 1, p. 466.
22. Holoman, p. 238.
23. Ibid., p. 144.
24. Tovey, *Essays in Musical Analysis*, vol. 4, pp. 74–75.
25. Bickley, "The concert overtures," p. 71.
26. Libbey, p. 694.
27. Cairns, vol. 2, p. 205.
28. Quoted in Holloman, p. 261.
29. Berlioz, *Memoirs*, p. 230.
30. Berlioz, *Roméo et Juliette*, Op.17, Introduction, p. x.
31. Cairns, *Berlioz*, vol. 2, p. 182.
32. Holoman, p. 260.
33. Dickinson, p. 133.

34. Berlioz, *Memoirs*, p. 125.
35. Quoted in Cairns, vol. 2, p. 357.
36. Berlioz, Preface to *La Damnation de Faust*, p. vii.
37. Ibid., p. 249.
38. Cairns, vol. 2, pp. 359–361.
39. Translation from D. Kern Holoman, p. 381.
40. James Haar, "The operas and dramatic legend," in *The Cambridge Companion to Berlioz*, ed. Peter Bloom, p. 91.
41. Berlioz, *Memoirs*, p. 37.
42. Ibid., p. 31.
43. Macdonald, program notes, p. 9.
44. *Oxford Dictionary of Music*, p. 594.
45. Berlioz, Te Deum, p. 1.
46. Holoman, pp. 516–-517.
47. Berlioz, Te Deum, p. 44.
48. See Cairns, *Berlioz*, vol. 2, pp. 553–555.
49. Holoman, pp. 521–523.
50. Barzun, v. 2, p. 169.
51. Berlioz, *L'Enfance du Christ*, p. 109.
52. Berlioz, *Memoirs*, pp. 209–210.
53. Ibid., p. 206.
54. Cairns, vol. 2, pp. 133–134.
55. Ibid., p. 135
56. Cone, *Berlioz's Divine Comedy: the Grande Messe des morts*, pp. 4–8.
57. Berlioz, *Requiem*, p. 9.
58. Cone, p. 10.
59. Ibid., pp. 13–14.
60. Berlioz, *Lelio*, p. 1.
61. Barzun, *Berlioz and the Romantic Century*, vol. 1, p. 150.
62. Holoman, p. 243.
63. Shakespeare, *The Tempest*, p. 2.
64. Holoman, p .191.
65. Julian Rushton, *St. James Opera Encyclopedia* entry on *Benvenuto Cellini*, pp. 77–78.
66. Haar, *The Operas and Dramatic Legends*, ed. Peter Bloom, p. 86.
67. Ibid., p. 88.
68. Holoman, p. 250.
69. *Ibid.*, p. 251
70. Haar, *The Operas and Dramatic Legends*, p. 88.
71. Holoman, p. 525.
72. Cairns, vol. 2, p. 599.

Notes 167

73. Dean, *"Les Troyens,"* p. 209.
74. Tovey, *Illustrative Music*, p. 89.
75. Holoman, p. 527.
76. Nelson, Introduction to *Les Troyens*, p. 33.
77. *Les Troyens*, libretto, pp. 111–112. Erato recordings, catalog no. 0190295762209.
78. Older recordings of *Les Troyens* sometimes substitute a French horn for the saxhorn. The darker, masculine tone of the saxhorn, here played offstage, works much better.
79. Haar, *The Cambridge Companion to Berlioz*, p. 93.
80. The couples mentioned by Shakespeare are: Troilus and Cressida; Pyramus and Thisbe; Dido and Aeneas.
81. See Holoman, p. 527.
82. Annegret Fraser, "The Songs," *The Cambridge Companion to Berlioz*, p. 119.
83. Holoman, p. 515.
84. Cairns, vol. 2, pp. 246–247.
85. Holoman, p. 515.
86. Barzun, vol. 2, p. 288.
87. List songs contain lists of items of some kind. Its greatest example on the classical side is the aria Madamina—My lady—from act 1 of Mozart's *Don Giovanni*, in which Leporello, the title character's servant, goes through a catalog listing his master's conquests. Popular music has many list songs as well. Cole Porter seems to have enjoyed writing them, because there are quite a few to his credit; "I Get a Kick Out of You" is probably the most famous. Most, although not all, in this category are cheerful demonstrations of wit, as demonstrated two of Bob Dylan's, "Subterranean Homesick Blues," which is satirical, but also the grim "A Hard Rain's a-Gonna Fall"

Selected Bibliography

Abbate, Carolyn, and Roger Parker. *A History of Opera*. New York: W. W. Norton, 2012.

Barzun, Jacques. *Berlioz and The Romantic Century*, vols. 1 and 2. Boston: Little, Brown and Co., 1950.

Berlioz, Hector. *Béatrice et Bénédict, Opéra-comique en 2 actes*. New York: Edwin F. Kalmus

Berlioz, Hector. *Evenings with the Orchestra*. Translated and edited by Jacques Barzun. Chicago: University of Chicago Press, reprinted 1999.

Berlioz, Hector. *La damnation de Faust, Dramatic Legend in Four Parts*. London: Ernst Eulenberg, 1964.

Berlioz, Hector. *Le Carnaval Romain, Overture for Orchestra*. London: Ernst Eulenberg, 1972.

Berlioz, Hector. *Le Corsaire, Overture for Orchestra*. London: Ernst Eulenberg, 1981.

Berlioz, Hector. *Lelio (The Return to Life)*. New York, Edwin F. Kalmus.

Berlioz, Hector. *L'Enfance du Christ*, Op. 25, Mineola, NY: Dover Publications, 1999.

Berlioz, Hector. *Les Francs Juges, Overture for Orchestra*. London: Ernst Eulenberg.

Berlioz, Hector. *Les nuits d'été*, Op. 7. Complete Song Cycle in Full Score and Vocal Score. Mineola, NY: Dover Publications, 2003.

Berlioz, Hector. *Les Troyens. Grand Opéra en cinq actes*. Vocal score. Kassel, Germany: Bärenreiter, 2003.

Berlioz, Hector. *Les Troyens*. Program notes accompanying complete opera conducted by John Nelson. Erato CD 019025762209.

Berlioz, Hector. *Memoirs of Hector Berlioz*. Translated, edited and introduced by David Cairns. London: Victor Gollancz, 1969.

Berlioz, Hector. *Requiem*, Op. 5 in Full Score. Mineola, NY: Dover Publications, 2006.

Berlioz, Hector. *Roméo et Juliette, Symphonie dramatique*, Op. 17. London: Ernst Eulenberg.

Berlioz, Hector. *Symphonie fantastique and Harold in Italy*. Full score, edited by Charles Malherbe and Felix Weingartner. Mineola, NY: Dover Publications, 1984.

Bloom, Peter, ed. *The Cambridge Companion to Berlioz*. Cambridge, UK: Cambridge University Press, 2000.

Cairns, David. *Berlioz: The Making of an Artist*. Berkeley: University of California Press, 2000.
Cairns, David. *Berlioz: Servitude and Greatness*. Berkeley: University of California Press, 2000.
Cone, Edward T. *Berlioz's Divine Comedy: the* Grande Messe des Morts. Paper published by University of California, 1980.
Dean, Winton. *Essays on Opera*. Oxford: Clarendon Paperbacks, 1990.
Dickinson, Alan E.F. *The Music of Berlioz*. New York: St, Martin's Press, 1972.
Guinn, John, and Les Stone, eds. *The St. James Opera Encyclopedia*. Detroit: Visible Ink Press, 1997.
Holoman, D. Kern. *Berlioz*. Cambridge, MA: Harvard University Press, 1989.
Kennedy, Michael, ed. *The Oxford Dictionary of Music*. 2nd ed. Oxford: Oxford University Press, 1994.
Kerman, Joseph. *Opera and the Morbidity of Music*. New York: New York Review Books, 2008.
Libbey, Ted. *The NPR Listeners' Encyclopedia of Classical Music*. New York: Workman Publishing, 2006.
Munch, Charles. *I Am a Conductor*. Translated by Leonard Burkat. New York: Oxford University Press, 1955.
Padgett, Ron, ed. *The Teachers and Writers Handbook of Poetic Forms*. New York: Teachers and Writers Collaborative, 1987.
Rosen, Charles. *The Romantic Generation*. Cambridge, MA: Harvard University Press, 1995.
Shakespeare, William. *The Tempest*, ed. Frank Kermode. London: Routledge, reprinted 1987.
Tovey, Donald Francis. *Essays in Musical Analysis, Vol. IV: Illustrative Music*, 5th ed. London: Oxford University Press, 1946.
Tovey, Donald Francis. *Essays in Musical Analysis, Vol. VI: Supplementary Essays*, 4th ed. London: Oxford University Press, 1945.
Tresize, Simon, ed. *The Cambridge Companion to French Music*. Cambridge, UK: Cambridge University Press, 2015.

Track Listing

Accompanying online audio is available at:
https://textbooks.rowman.com/berlioz-listener

1. *Symphonie fantastique*, first movement. Lyon National Orchestra, conducted by Leonard Slatkin (14.37).
2. Roman Carnival Overture. Polish State Philharmonic Orchestra, Katowice, conducted by Kenneth Jean (8:46).
3. *Roméo et Juliette,* part 2, *Scène d'amour.* Lyon National Orchestra, conducted by Leonard Slatkin (16.31).
4. *La Damnation de Faust,* part 3. *Autrefois un Roi de Thulé*, Marie-Ange Todorovich as Marguerite; Orchestre Nationale de Lille, conducted by Jean-Claude Casadesus (4:22).
5. *La Damnation de Faust*, part 4. *Nature immense* ("Invocation to Nature"), Michael Myers as Faust; Orchestre Nationale de Lille, conducted by Jean-Claude Casadesus (4:13).
6. *La Damnation de Faust,* part 4. *La Course à l'Abîme* (The Ride to the Abyss). Michael Myers as Faust; Alain Vernhes as Méphistophélès; Orchestre Nationale de Lille, conducted by Jean-Claude Casadesus (3:39).
7. Requiem (*Grand Messe des Morts*). Lacrimosa. Elora Festival Orchestra, Toronto Mendelssohn Choir, Toronto Mendelssohn Youth Choir, conducted by Noel Edison (9:45).
8. *Au Cimetière (Clair de Lune)*, from *Les Nuits d'Été*. Soile Isokoski, mezzo-soprano, Helsingin kaupunginorkesteri, conducted by John Storgårds (5:05).
9. *L'Île inconnue*, from *Les Nuits d'Été*. Soile Isokoski, mezzo-soprano, Helsingin kaupunginorkesteri, conducted by John Storgårds (4:11).

Recordings are licensed under permission of Naxos of America, Inc.
℗ Naxos of America, Inc.

www.ingramcontent.com/pod-product-compliance
Lightning Source LLC
Chambersburg PA
CBHW070831300426
44111CB00014B/2521